Every Nursery Needs a Garden

'If outdoor activities with young children have always baffled you then this is the book for you. Practical in style and structure, it has an accessible approach that is based in the best early years practice and provides plenty of challenges and new ideas. It is a must-have for your early years setting.'

Kathryn Solly, Head Teacher at Chelsea Open Air Nursery School
and Children's Centre, UK

A garden can be a magical place for young children and offers them rich and engaging learning experiences as they interact with a variety of plants and wildlife throughout the year. This book guides you through the process of creating a garden, however small, for young children. It looks at the impact a garden area can have on children's overall development and the benefits of using natural materials as learning tools.

Full of practical advice on how to design, develop, resource and use a garden area, this book brings together:

- advice on planning a garden and how to get children, parents and the local community involved
- ideas for settings with limited space
- ideas for different spaces including a wildlife space, a woodland space, a digging area, sand and water spaces and a growing area
- suggestions of plants, flowers and crops to grow with very young children
- information about the wildlife that children may discover
- a calendar guide to activities and garden planning throughout the year
- ways to encourage children to develop a sense of awareness of the importance of conservation and sustainability
- guidance on health and safety

- clear links with EYFS to show how a garden supports the areas of learning and development.

Written for all early years practitioners, this book is the definitive guide for those looking to further enhance their outdoor environment and fulfil the potential learning opportunities that a garden can provide.

Ann Watts is an early years consultant with many years' experience both as a nursery class teacher and head teacher. She is an accredited facilitator and trainer for Learning through Landscapes and advises early years settings and schools in developing their outdoor areas.

Every Nursery Needs a Garden

A step-by-step guide to creating and using a garden with young children

Ann Watts

Routledge
Taylor & Francis Group

LONDON AND NEW YORK

This first edition published 2011
by Routledge
2 Park Square, Milton Park, Abingdon, Oxon, OX14 4RN

Simultaneously published in the USA and Canada
by Routledge
711 Third Avenue, New York, NY 10017

Routledge is an imprint of the Taylor & Francis Group, an informa business

Typeset in Bembo by
Pindar NZ, Auckland, New Zealand
Printed and bound in Great Britain by
TJ Internatinal Ltd, Padstow, Cornwall

British Library Cataloguing in Publication Data
A catalogue record for this book is available from the British Library

Library of Congress Cataloging-in-Publication Data
Watts, Ann.
Every nursery needs a garden / Ann Watts. — 1st ed.
    p. cm.
    Includes bibliographical references and index.
    1. Children's gardens. 2. Child development. 3. Early childhood education. I. Title.
    SB457.W38 2011
    372.35'7—dc22   2010046661

ISBN13: 978-0-415-59130-0 (hbk)
ISBN13: 978-0-415-59131-7 (pbk)
ISBN13: 978-0-203-81849-7 (ebk)

Contents

This book is dedicated to
Joshua, Harry and Lucy,
a continual source of pleasure and inspiration,
as they worked and played in gardens.

I would like to express grateful thanks also to the staff, parents and children of the following settings, for kindly allowing me to visit and giving me permission to take and use photographs for this book.

Chelsea Open Air Nursery School
Chertsey Nursery School
Crosfield Nursery School
Epsom Downs Primary School
KISH Kindergarten
Major Minors Day Nursery
Nutfield Day Nursery
Peter Pan Preschool Nursery
Playbox St Johns Preschool Nursery
Purley Nursery school
St Ives School
St Michael's Community Nursery
Stagecoach Montesssori Nursery

Garden calendar

January

- Observe and pick snowdrops.
- Provide high-quality materials, paints, pastels and chalks for children to draw and paint them.
- Collect dried seed heads – use to make musical instruments or other art work.
- Buy flower and vegetable seeds and seed potatoes.
- Put food and water out for birds.
- Observe winter bark – make rubbings.

February

- Look out for catkins and other developing buds and shoots.
- Chit potatoes by putting them into egg boxes with eyes at the top; leave in a cool dry light place.

March

- Plan time to observe and draw spring bulbs, measure height each week.
- Plant early potatoes.
- Add compost to vegetable beds.
- Sow tomato seeds and keep indoors.
- Sow carrot seeds in ground or large pot.
- Look under log piles for wildlife; record findings.

April

- Sow peas and sweet peas in individual pots.
- Sow beans, courgettes and any other crops according to instructions on packet.

- Sow lettuces in trays.
- Sow wildflower seeds in trays or in ground.
- Sow sunflowers in newspaper pots.
- Check all seeds regularly and water as necessary.
- Observe wildlife, feed birds and check for nest building.

May

- Make a scarecrow for the vegetable plot.
- Plant out French and runner beans, lettuces, courgettes and any other vegetable.
- Plant out peas and sweet peas.
- Provide supports for peas, sweet peas, beans and tomatoes.
- Buy and plant out any bedding plants.
- Water regularly.

June

- Water, water, water.
- Check for weeds around crops.
- Observe dragonflies and other insects.
- Check under log piles.
- Sow carrots to harvest in September.
- Pick herbs and use in role play and cooking.

July

- Pick sweet peas and arrange in small vases.
- Harvest onions, potatoes and salad crops.
- Harvest early tomatoes and beans.
- Pick and eat strawberries.
- Plan cooking activities to use fresh produce.
- Arrange for someone to care for garden if setting is closed in August.

August

- Harvest carrots, runner beans and tomatoes.
- Keep watering!

September

- Draw and measure height of sunflowers.
- Harvest crops.

- Plant spring bulbs in ground and/or containers.
- Observe spider webs on bushes.

October

- Observe changing colours of leaves on shrubs and trees.
- Collect fallen leaves and autumn fruits and use for different activities.
- Plant alliums and lilies.
- Check shrubs, remove unwanted growth and buy new bushes if necessary.
- Plant new trees.
- Harvest pumpkins – think of ways of transporting them back to the class-room, count seeds and make soup.
- Plant tulip bulbs.

November

- Sweep leaves and put into composting bags to make leaf mould.
- Find worms to add to the compost bin.
- Keep bird feeders topped up.
- Protect any tender plants for winter; introduce conversations about animals hibernating.

December

- Continue to provide food and water for birds.
- Make a Christmas tree for wildlife.
- Decorate trees or shrubs with fairy lights.
- Make decorations out of natural materials using Oasis glue and glitter.
- Decorate small fir trees and use as gifts.

Introduction

There has been a strong focus in recent years on letting children play outside and creating learning opportunities outdoors. Recent terminology refers to outdoor classrooms, outdoor spaces or learning environments, but very few texts focus on the garden itself as being a central force in children's learning.

This book has come about as a natural combination of my love of gardening and many years' experience working with young children. In particular, I have always enjoyed being outside with children and I have come to realize that the environment itself can have a profound impact on the quality of children's play and consequently their learning and development.

I have been fortunate to be able to lead a project where children and staff worked together to transform a tarmac playground into a nursery garden. Children who lived in flats were able to run and climb freely, but also began to experience the joys of being surrounded by plants and trees of many kinds, using them in their play and as a stimulus for their questions, their fascinations and curiosities. Since then I have worked with many other settings and found that practitioners are full of enthusiasm for making a garden space but always welcome support to give them the confidence to manage a project.

The book has three main aims. First, it will challenge head teachers, managers, practitioners and students to think creatively about the ways children use outdoor spaces and about how the spaces can be planned to provide a rich environment for children in their first six years. It focuses on the idea that, in addition to a dedicated growing space, children need gardens from a very early age.

Second, it will offer practical support to all early years practitioners wishing to develop a garden, however small, for their children. It highlights the importance of creating a garden space wherever possible, so children can become directly involved with plants and wildlife.

There is practical advice about setting up and planning a project and detailed suggestions for the types of imaginative spaces you might wish to include for your children. This is followed by advice on the types of plants that could be used in a garden layout, and also tips and suggestions for growing plants and vegetables with very young children. As well as ideas for planting and growing in larger spaces, the book gives ideas for indoor or window box gardening for childminders, and ideas for settings that use shared spaces.

The third aim is to encourage practitioners to use not just the growing section but the whole garden, as a teaching resource. Being out in a garden with young children offers an incredible range of learning opportunities for everyone. Children observe first hand and will ask questions about what they see. One chapter details ways of using and maintaining the garden with an emphasis on the need to recycle and care for our natural world and the following chapter gives a brief description of what can be found in a garden. This is followed by links to the Early Years Foundation Stage (EYFS), showing how from the very beginning of a project you can encapsulate all four themes of EYFS. There are also ideas and advice showing how the garden can be used to promote learning and development in all six areas of learning.

Four case studies relate first-hand experience of setting up and using gardens or working outdoors with children. They include a nursery school that created a garden on a piece of tarmac, and a day nursery that tackled a hugely overgrown site and made a children's garden. There is an observation of children planting with coir in a preschool in shared premises and an observation of a forest school activity run from a playgroup. Suggestions are given for ways to include something of the forest school ethos in a setting without a woodland space. These are available online at www.routledge.com/teachers/resources/fulton.

I hope this book will inspire readers to become excited and confident enough to translate their ideas into practice and create vibrant and exciting gardens for their children. This, in turn, will enable the children themselves to develop what could be a lifelong interest and relationship with the natural world and an awareness of their own role within it.

1

Why do young children need gardens?

Introduction

Today, there is an ever-growing trend towards living and working in garden environments. 'Grow your own' is a common catchphrase, and many popular television programmes feature gardening, wildlife and food.

What is so special about a garden? It is essentially a living, growing environment that responds, as we do, to the seasons, and it can offer a place for increasing knowledge; for work and relaxation; and developing a sense of awe and spiritual awareness. The Oxford English Dictionary definition of a garden is an 'enclosed piece of ground devoted to the cultivation of flowers, fruit or vegetables'. A wider use of the term, however, would also include the growing trend for wild gardens and meadow areas, as well as the relationship between the land and owner. If we see our children as 'owners' of the land they occupy on a daily basis, we will be able to observe this relationship and understand its significance.

Many primary and secondary schools now offer gardening clubs and time for children to be outdoors. Therefore, it seems natural that we should be looking at ways of setting up garden spaces for our younger children. I believe if we are to do this successfully, we need to understand some of the historical background of gardens for young children and also the current thinking that may define our approach.

Historical background

The importance of a garden for young children was first recognized by Friedrich Froebel in 1899. He devised the word 'kindergarten', which is still very much in use today. Literally translated it means 'children's garden'. He believed that, through tending to plants, a child came to an awareness of the needs of others. Children should be very much in union with nature, and working in the garden was an important part of the daily pattern. Children learnt how to write their names as they labelled their garden plots. They learnt how to count and measure, as they cut out uniform flower and vegetable beds, sowed seeds in rows and collected crops. There appears to be a large gap in any recorded practice of children learning in gardens after that. Similar mathematical learning was not recorded in the UK until the middle of the 1970s. Parry and Archer (1975) wrote about a group of children who wanted to establish their own garden and carefully measured the rows, spaced the seeds and counted the number of days it took for the seeds to appear and then develop.

Margaret McMillan (1923) established open air nursery schools in the UK and described in detail the classroom 'roofed only by the sky'. She was keen to develop the children's senses. She planted herbs, trees and flowers in profusion. She realized the garden was an instructive environment and devised a curriculum of relevance. She used the design features of the garden to provide opportunities for physical development, low walls, tree trunks, logs and stepping stones so that 'children were encouraged to play bravely and adventurously' (McMillan 1919: 23). Her garden could also be used as a place for telling stories and performing plays. She advocated the use of clay and paint outside and the illustrations in her book contained images of children dancing and making music in the garden (McMillan 1930).

Scientific and technological development also seemed to occur naturally in the garden environment of the pioneers. Froebel (1899), McMillan (1919) and Isaacs (1954) describe how children should use tools. The planting of seeds, observation of growth and looking for mini-beasts were all an important part of the curriculum. The pioneers noticed how children were naturally attracted to the outdoors and Tizard (1976) noticed that in a free play situation children would choose to spend 75 per cent of their time outside. Their level of play was more complex and mature than when indoors.

During the 1980s, although there was an increase in provision for children under five, gardening in our schools and nurseries was, at best, an indoor 'planting in yogurt pots' experience. Outdoor play focused on physical activity and provision often consisted of a climbing frame, a sandpit and a few bikes. The word 'garden' so frequently used by Froebel, McMillan and other Early

Years educators disappeared as the nursery school movement extended and was replaced by terms such as playground, outdoor play space or 'outside area'.

Benefits of a garden for young children

Educationalists are now realizing once more how important it is for children to spend as much time as possible outside, particularly in their early years.

Richard Louv (2005) believes that children today are suffering from what he calls 'nature deficit disorder'. He presents a compelling argument that regular contact with nature is important for physical and mental health. He cites examples of some of the nature-based childhood activities of some of the greatest creative thinkers of our times. He believes that when children have hands-on experiences with nature, they reap the benefits. He has found that researchers cite diminishment in levels of attention deficit hyperactivity disorder (ADHD), fewer incidents of anxiety and depression, improved self-esteem, enhanced brain development, higher levels of curiosity and creativity, and a sense of connectedness to the community and the environment. In his book, *Last Child in the Woods*, he interviews children, teachers and parents. His plea for allowing children access to the outdoors has kick-started a movement in America called 'Leave No Child Inside'.

Children in the UK, too, are growing up in a society where they spend less time outdoors. Many live in urban housing and do not have access to any outdoor play space. Some may go to a park and play on swings, but they do not have that special place where they have ownership, where they can pick up sticks, explore the mud, stand under trees, listen to wavy grasses rustling and feel the breeze on their skin. They are not able to splash in mud or dig in soil. There is a higher incidence of asthma in young children, and Michie and Bangalor (2010) report that some children now suffer vitamin D deficiency as a result of lack of exposure to sunshine.

Marjorie Ouvry (2005) emphasizes the importance of children spending as much time as possible outside. In 'Outdoors for Everyone' (Ouvry 2009) she describes 'the special nature' of the outdoors. We need to consider in more detail what is meant by this. Outdoor play should include some interaction with the natural environment, and enable adults and children to become deeply involved with the environment itself, as well as the artefacts within it. Ferre Leavers *et al.* (2005) have been studying the relationship between children's involvement and their well-being. They have devised a scale that clearly shows how children's well-being depends on self-esteem and confidence and is linked to their ability to become involved in activities at a deeper level.

Involvement means that you are completely open to experiences: the impressions you get are very strong. Bodily sensations and movements, colours and sounds, smells and tastes have a certain range and depth that is not there otherwise. You fully address your fantasy and mental capabilities. When involvement is low the sensations are not really lived through and remain superficial (2005: 10).

A garden will provide the chance for children to find themselves, to enjoy physical and mental challenge, but also be able to be calm, have personal space and interact with nature.

White and Stoeklin (1998) argue that it is essential that young children are allowed to develop empathy with nature by playing in a natural environment on a regular basis. They develop a love of nature or biophilia, which, in time, will enable them to be in tune with wider issues of conservation on a global basis. They argue that if children have not experienced this empathy at an early age, they cannot then understand or cope with these wider issues and may even develop a phobia about issues concerning the natural world.

Current thinking

White and Stoeklin (1998) go on to suggest that some of the most developmentally appropriate environments are seen in the forest schools of Scandinavia, where young children spend almost all of their time outdoors. In Scotland, there is one nursery that operates within an outdoor forest setting all the time. Forest schools are now being set up across the UK and children will be able to attend, usually for a prescribed block of time. During this time, they work with specially trained adults to learn skills of survival and are able to interact with the natural environment in a deeper and meaningful way. Sara Knight (2009) writes about this in detail and also suggests that, although we cannot create forests in our settings, we may be able to introduce the ethos of forest school into our work.

Many children in primary schools are reaping the benefits of carefully planned spaces supervised by adults who can support their learning. The Royal Horticultural Society (RHS) has set up a very successful national campaign for school gardens. Children are encouraged to work outdoors and grow plants and vegetables as part of a healthier lifestyle. They are taught about the benefits of a good diet and this will go some way to combating the problems of obesity in children. However, this learning needs to start with our youngest children.

Garden spaces for babies and toddlers, as well as children in nursery and reception classes, need to be carefully planned.

When practitioners attend training to consider outdoor spaces, I often ask them to talk about what they would like outside for the children if there were no financial constraints or problems of space. Without exception, they present plans of what can only be termed as a 'children's garden'. They think of winding tracks and paths, different textures and levels, grass, hillocks and secret corners. There are stepping stones, splash areas, rocks, waterfalls, safe pools and sand areas. There is usually a growing area and a separate space for children to just dig, turn over logs and explore. One group listed herbs and plants they would include. Species can be chosen for their sensuous appeal and their attraction to birds and insects. There are spaces set aside for music, for telling stories, acting out plays, reading books and painting. There is room to run and shout, to watch the clouds and listen to birdsong. There are also natural and man-made materials and objects that can be used to recreate and represent children's own ideas and imaginary situations.

Conclusion

Our educational thinking has moved forward and many settings are successfully managing free-flow situations. Practitioners are beginning to see the indoors and outdoors as linked areas and make appropriate provision for learning. Staff can feel under additional pressure as they have to move more equipment and apparatus outside on a daily basis. A well-designed and established garden presents a readymade 'classroom' and reduces the need for this. Children can access the area for short or long periods of time as they wish and have the freedom to play, explore and develop their own interests.

If we really believe that children need to be outside, we need to examine what we are offering in our schools and early years settings. We must make the most of the opportunities and the spaces that we have. Children need to develop an awareness of the seasons, a concern for the natural environment and knowledge of plant growth. These things can only be done if the outdoor space is carefully planned and adults are willing to respond to the children's interests and experiences. Once this development and transformation of your outdoor space begins, children and staff will enjoy the garden together and benefit from the learning opportunities it provides.

2

How do we make a garden?

Introduction

In this chapter, I will attempt to answer some of the most common questions asked by practitioners and hope that even the faint-hearted among you become inspired to meet this challenge. There is no one answer, for every single nursery and reception space is different. The focus is on setting up and managing a project over time, which will enhance your outdoor space. It includes some of the problems common to many settings and sets out some ideas and practical solutions that can be adapted to your own environment. In the following chapter, there will be more detailed suggestions for the types of spaces you might wish to include.

The essential element to any major development in any setting is, from the start, to involve the staff, the children, the parents, any external managers or stake holders, and members of the local community.

Getting started

It is important to plan in stages, and work towards a long-term vision. A garden does not happen overnight – except maybe on *Groundforce*. Even then, many hours of planning and preparation will have taken place before they start. It is important to think big. Many settings have embarked on improving a small patch of ground without thinking of the area as a whole and then have had to move it or change it as other ideas emerged. Thinking about costs can be a great inhibitor to creativity, so it is important to encourage staff to think about ideals and risk-taking. Very often, if there is a large-scale plan carefully worked out, it can be achieved in small stages. Careful planning and inspired thinking will attract funding. Children and adults can become very adept at encouraging people to give when it is needed. It is worth thinking whether a parent could help by making phone calls and visits to ask for support in different places in the local community. If possible, find out whether there are any other settings in your area that have developed their garden space. Arrange to visit if possible, and ask about any difficulties they encountered as well as learning about their success.

Managing a project

Try to establish a small group to act as a management team. It should represent different sections of your staffing profile, parents, community link person, committee member or governors. This means that workload can be shared and any long-term plans are not affected by a change in personnel. Identify key roles, e.g. project leader, fund raiser, project finance and project information coordinator. Try to meet regularly to ensure momentum is not lost. Set timescales. You will need a long-term scale and within that, work out short-term scales, i.e. what can you do in the next six months, the next year, etc. It may be that some goals will only be achieved if there is sufficient funding, but timescales can always be adapted to meet needs.

Involving the children

From the very beginning of any development, however small, it is essential that the children feel that they are involved in planning the garden. This ensures that they feel it is a special place for them. A short film about gardens can be shown to encourage their thinking. Some children may have gardens at home and be able to describe what they like doing in the garden. A nursery visit to any nearby gardens, garden centre or allotments would give an excellent starting point for their thinking. Library books or gardening magazines provide lots of coloured pictures. It is usually possible to get a group ticket from a library, which allows you to borrow a greater number of books. Raid the gardening section and try putting these books out for a day in the children's book boxes and shelves. Plan to have one or two adults available to observe and interact with children. Record their conversations and note what elements appeal to

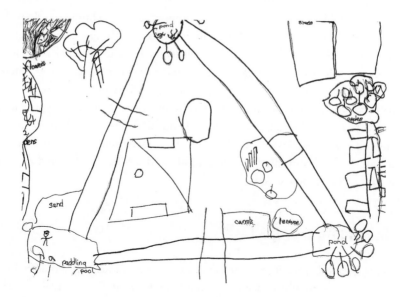

Figure 2.1 Children's drawings and ideas should be included in a design brief. This five-year-old wanted three ponds and bridges to connect them as well as a den and somewhere to grow carrots.

them. Discussion can focus on what plants appeal to them, which vegetables and why we grow them. Children will look closely at elements of design, textured paving, ponds, wildlife areas and water features. Ask parents or grandparents to save flower catalogues and gardening magazines. Children could look through these, and cut out things that appeal to them. It is important from the very beginning to keep a focus on the plants and planting as this is, after all, what will transform your space into a garden. Use the cut-outs of plants, vegetables, features and design elements to build a collage or picture board. Alternatively, you could have a large site plan available and the pictures could be glued onto it. This can be made into a display for parents and visitors to see.

One school made a large paper tree and each child took home a paper cut-out apple. They discussed at home with their parents what feature they would like to see in their outdoor space, wrote it on the apple, and brought it back to school to hang on the tree. This then became a focus for the parents group as they began to raise funds.

Observing children

Observing children's behaviour from a very early age will give you clues as to what they enjoy outside. Edwards *et al.*'s (1998) *The Hundred Languages of*

Children describes how young babies use their bodies to indicate their needs, as they turn to look out of the window, or watch leaves moving in the sunlight. Try giving children a soft toy to take outside – maybe Paddington Bear who comes complete with wellies. Ask them what Paddington would like to do in a garden and use their ideas.

The organization, Learning through Landscapes, uses any available items to represent new garden features; e.g. blue fabric could be a pond, sticks could be laid out to simulate a log walk and cones could mark out pathways. This exercise, called 'Planning for Real' is described in detail in a Playnotes leaflet (available from Learning through Landscapes).

The 'mosaic approach' devised by Clark and Moss (2001) asks groups of children to use a camera outside to record spaces they particularly like, and then discuss the pictures in more depth.

Involving the parents

Share your enthusiasm and encourage parents to contribute ideas and practical help. If possible, plan a meeting at a time convenient to the majority. Ask parents to think about their own childhood and what they enjoyed or remember. Very often, they will talk about having hours of freedom, digging in mud, making rose petal perfume, building dens, lighting fires and climbing trees. These are some of the rich childhood experiences that have contributed to their own development, and it is very likely they will want to pass these on to their children. Without a garden in the safe confines of the nursery environment this may not be possible. Consider ways to involve parents from different cultures and help them to understand the importance of this project and how it will help their children.

Development day

Plan a day where adults, all staff and as many parents as can attend can meet together to share ideas and concepts. Before this, circulate information about the day and ask them to come prepared to share ideas of what they would like in the outdoor area. Suggest that they look at garden magazines and cut out any pictures that appeal to them. An image board can be displayed in the entrance hall or main notice board. Parents and children can add to this image board. Buy some of the books in the 'further reading and useful resources' section of this chapter, lend them out and discuss some ideas about whether children need gardens and why this is different from just a playground space.

Table 2.1 Outline plan for development day

Morning session	■ Initial discussion about play spaces that adults enjoyed when they were children
	■ Discuss what experiences you would like to offer children outside
	■ Staff member to present the children's ideas, sharing drawings and conversations
	■ Brainstorm ideas of 'spaces for learning' (see next section). It might be useful to summarize these for everyone to see before you meet
	■ Explore any issues or concerns, e.g. health and safety, children's clothing, being outside in all weathers. Write up on flow chart; list barriers and ways to overcome them
Afternoon session	■ Provide large sheets with outline of existing boundaries
	■ Adults work in small groups to make a basic outline plan of their ideas. Write in ideas of any textured surfaces and plants that could be used
	■ List any other areas they might like to include but couldn't fit into the design. Collate plans and agree next steps, whether to consult a professional or continue 'in house'

Working with a professional

If you are considering employing an architect or designer, consider joining the Learning through Landscapes organization and follow the appropriate links on their website (available online at www.learningthroughlandscapes.org.uk). Also, local authority advisory staff may be able to offer support. A third party can be a useful sounding board or may be able to suggest other avenues of help. Parents could suggest local landscape designers that they know, but always check references and make sure you know whether they can meet your needs before agreeing to any fees. However, it is important that you choose someone you feel you can work with. If you are not happy with any particular aspect of the design it is important that you can communicate this. You are the people who work on the site with the children. You are the professionals in child development and you know best what is appropriate for their learning. You need to find someone who is happy to work with the ideas you have had, rather than superimposing their own grand designs.

Audit skills

Developing a garden involves many skills (not just a love of gardening), and a skills audit of staff, parents and community helpers is a good way forward. A request letter could be sent out suggesting what is needed. List the following areas where you may need help: building, DIY, painting, carpentry, gardening, letter writing, fundraising, and contacting local community groups. Find out where parents work. Maybe they could raise support from their workplace, particularly if it is local.

Funding

This is one of the biggest areas to consider. 'We'd love to do something outside but we haven't got any money!' is a common cry, but the people making this statement need to gather a team of supporters and come up with their ideas and vision plan. Once this is achieved, then it is time to start thinking about the money. Each part of the overall plan can be costed as an individual section and fundraising can start. People are much more likely to contribute if they can see exactly what they are giving money for. Detailed sketches and an outline of how any particular area will contribute to the learning and development of the children will inspire parents and other stakeholders to offer support.

At the time of writing, different grants are available from local authorities to develop outdoor spaces. Consider your space carefully, as any application for a grant needs to meet certain criteria. Before you start any application, read through it carefully and ensure that you respond to each section and give evidence for each of their listed criteria. It is a time-consuming process, but an essential part of your ultimate success. Also, make sure you complete any application at least a week before the actual deadline. *Set yourself an early completion date.* This ensures your application will get to the right place in time.

Often, you will need to include in your application evidence that you have involved children and families. Not only will they need to be involved in the actual design, but also play an essential part in the fundraising process. Children will enjoy making cakes or gifts to sell, and if this is done regularly over a period of time, money will accrue.

It is important always to maintain an overall vision of the whole design plan, but at the same time this can be broken down into sections for costings. It may be that there is only enough money to build a wildlife area this year, but another area can be built when funds become available. Learning through Landscapes provides a very useful and comprehensive list of funding sources and ideas.

If you are considering using a professional contractor always get estimates from three companies. These need to be carefully checked. In one nursery school, one of the governors with some architectural experience discovered that three estimates gave very different measurements for the ground area required, let alone different prices for the work.

Designing the garden: first considerations

Whenever you make important decisions, always ask yourselves the question, 'What type of experiences do we want to offer our children?'.

Fixed play equipment

Many settings have access to a space that already contains some storage and play equipment. In many cases there is a large fixed climbing frame or slide. Sometimes, the only reason for keeping this is because it might upset the parents who paid for it ten years ago. Talk through this issue in depth, and often you will find that many people say it actually gets in the way and children only get limited play opportunity. In most cases, it is advisable to take down anything that is likely to impede the natural flow of the space. Look closely at the ways the children use the equipment. Do they use it when there is little else for them to do or is it an important part of their daily play even when the area is richly resourced with other play opportunities?

It is vitally important that children are given opportunities for a wide range of physical movement, but there are many ways of planning for this without the need for very large and expensive fixed frames. Some playground companies offer a variety of challenging trail equipment, swing bridges and log walks. They can fit into smaller spaces or round the perimeter without dominating the central area. Large climbing structures need to have a clear space of two metres around them as a critical fall height. This again leaves an area of unusable space. Many settings have small outdoor areas and there is the need to fit in provision for a wide range of activities as well as leaving free space for ball play or wheeled vehicles. At one time outdoor play was dominated by tricycles, but now many settings are able to incorporate this as part of a richer provision.

Existing natural features

Make the most of any natural features you already have. If there are large trees you will have instant shade. Think about the best ways to use the space under the trees. Many parks and playgrounds have put seating around a tree. However, this is rather unnatural and does not encourage communication, as children will be sitting looking away from each other. Instead, think about adding some more natural compost or bark around the tree. Once it is established children will be able to use this as a natural area to look for mini-beasts. Some old logs could be added and, if possible, provide some upturned logs for children to sit on.

Think too about whether any large trees could be used for a tree house. If there are large trees, it is a wise investment to ask a tree specialist to examine them to see if they are safe. Falling branches can be lethal. A tree house needs to be carefully designed and a risk assessment completed. Good design will eliminate any possible dangers and the joy of having their own private space gives children something very special.

Look at the ways any trees you have can offer opportunities for movement and climbing. It may be possible to import a large tree trunk. Contact local landscape contractors. A suitable tree trunk lying on the ground gives opportunities for children to climb, swing and jump, as well as develop their imaginative skills.

If you have large bushes or hedges, look critically at them and see whether they could be used, with some careful pruning, to make hidey holes or dens for the children. Internal stems or trunks might be removed to leave a space that only a small child can access, and the foliage makes a natural roof and walls.

Storage spaces

These need to be considered right at the beginning of all projects. Any existing storage needs to be audited. Is it easily accessible for staff and children? Is it adequate? What is the life expectancy of the building or shed? Assess whether it is worth repairing or whether it may be better to invest more money and start again. Most settings say there is never enough storage space, so increasing this may need to be an integral part of your plan. Some nurseries have built a garage in a corner of their space so that all resources can be put out and away with minimal effort. Children are then able to access resources safely as they need them. Sometimes the side of a building can be roofed and a door put in, so bicycles and wheeled toys can be stored separately from other resources.

Surveying your site

In addition to writing down your ideas and drawing up a basic site plan, it is important to check with your local authority or site owner to see whether there are any restrictions on development. Normally, planning permission is not required to erect small storage, but if you were thinking of building a garage, you would need planning permission. You will also need to find out the location of gas and water services, and also any drainage systems.

Where to go for help

Learning through Landscapes has a very useful database of professionals who can help with any outdoor project. There are landscape designers as well as early years professionals, who have wide experience in working with children in EYFS and are particularly interested in outdoor learning. A visit by one of these can provide you with more ideas and also a printed report, which can be very useful – especially if you are applying to other places for funding.

Consider making links with a nearby secondary school. Pupils there sometimes need to work on practical projects as part of their study. It may be that a group would be able to work in your setting to help with some of the basic groundwork as well as possibly working with your pupils. Some settings have embarked on joint art projects where children of different ages have worked together on a mural or sculpture.

Maintaining your garden

Even though you have not yet built your garden, you need to plan right from the beginning how you will maintain any improvements you make. Timescales and costings need to be thought about. Maintenance is an important part of managing safety. It is a good idea to make a list or a chart of features that need regular maintenance tasks. Build any ongoing costs into your annual budget.

Staff training

As you move forward in your thinking about outdoor provision, it is important to consider what is available for professional development of staff. Managers might benefit from training on how to manage a project, or maybe, how to provide challenge and manage risk. Other practitioners might benefit from

Table 2.2 Example of maintenance chart

Item	What needs to be done	When	How much might it cost?	Who will do it?
Sandpit	Check for hazards/ cleanliness	Every day	Nothing	Outdoor key person
	Replace/top up sand	Once a year spring time	£100	Contractor
Wooden walkways	Check fixings	Daily	Nothing	Staff
	Apply preservative to woodwork	Every three years	£200	Contractor
Garden tidiness	Easy weeding	Every week in summer	Nothing	Children and staff/parents
	Pruning of large shrubs or trees	Late autumn	£150	Contract gardener

the many courses on offer on outdoor play and learning. The role of the adult outdoors was sometimes seen as monitoring or 'supervising' play. Now, we understand how adults are needed to support even the child–initiated activities and how, by observing these and acting on our observations, we can further extend children's learning. *Plan course fees into your budget costs for the project!*

Celebrate success

As your garden nears completion, it is important to think about how you might celebrate your development. It may be just a small section of a garden or a larger space. An 'official' opening attracts publicity for your setting and every-one who has been involved in the project should feel valued. Maybe a special event could be held which, in turn, might generate even more funding for future developments. Contact the local newspaper and invite the neighbours. An attractive garden space will often appeal to prospective new families and encourage them to register, particularly if there is information displayed about the ways it will benefit young children.

Further reading and useful resources

Learning through Landscapes information:

> Learning through Landscapes
> Southside
> The Law Courts
> Winchester SO23 9DL Tel: 01962 845811
>
> By subscribing to this organisation you will be able to download many useful resources from their website. Early Years Outdoors offers 'Playnotes'. Look at 'Developing New Spaces' November 2007, 'Planning for Real', 'Groundnotes', 'Working with Landscape Architects' and members' advice sheet 'Funding your School Ground Development'. Available online at www.ltl.org.uk

'Outdoors for Everyone' CD-Rom toolkit. This resource can be used to inform staff or parents about the vision for Early Years Outdoors. Obtainable from Learning through Landscapes.

Ryder Richardson, G. (2008) *Creating a Space to Grow.* Abingdon: David Fulton. There is a good section in this book on developing your outdoor space and ways to involve children.

Sargent, J. (2009) comp. *Without Walls: Creative Work with Families Developing and Using Outdoor Space.* Available from Learning through Landscapes or earlyyearspublications@oxfordshire.gov.uk. This gives practical advice, including how to build a sandpit, and information on forest school activities.

3

Garden spaces for children

Introduction

A really challenging, creative outdoor space will include opportunities for children to experience nature at first hand, and opportunities to develop their own play and learning by accessing a range of natural and man-made materials. The space should allow children to actively manipulate their environment, and encourage them to engage in quiet as well as active play. There might be landmarks and beautiful objects that create a sense of place and give children clear messages about how much they are valued. Ideally, there will be grass, plants and trees, and diverse textures and spaces for children to explore and alter as the mood takes them. There will be small pathways, and places to be alone or with friends.

When you have worked together and brainstormed your initial ideas, have a look at the following sections. These are the spaces most commonly suggested for inclusion in any overall design.

Spaces for babies and toddlers

There is a wide range of provision in the UK for very young children and it is important to give thought to the outdoor space for them. They may access the same space as older children or have a separate area. If they access the same space, it is important that there are some areas within that space that are specifically

Figure 3.1 Babies love exploring different textures. This toddler delights in touching soft moss.

designed to meet the needs of younger children. This will enable staff to relax and focus on observing the children and develop meaningful exploration.

In your setting, take some time to consider the benefits for the youngest children of being outside in a garden. Discuss how long babies should be outside, whether they go out in all weathers and what they can do in a garden. Talk about what you consider safe for babies, remembering that what presents a risk for one child may not be a risk for another. Younger babies are often calmed by the movements of leaves and trees and will respond to different textures of plants around them. As they become more mobile, consider whether you can present changes in floor levels, a small slope, stepping stones sunk into the ground or low-level steps. Different floor textures could be used for different parts of a 'baby space'. Toddlers enjoy moving things around and will become totally absorbed by a muddy puddle or some large pebbles. Long grass provides a different experience and also an area of moss gives another interesting texture. Raised grassy banks, logs or sunken tyres can give opportunities for babies to pull themselves up. They need to be able to explore, to walk or crawl into small spaces. Think about bamboo screens or bushes that give this hideaway feel.

Wildlife space

Nowadays, there is a very strong focus on biodiversity and the need to balance our environment so plants and animals can live in harmony. If our children are to grow up with an understanding of the need to care for our world, the best place to start is in their foundation stage setting. There, they will be able to absorb the knowledge and skills that the adults provide on a daily basis.

If there is no access to outdoors in your setting, it is essential to find somewhere to take the children to experience firsthand the ways that birds, butterflies and insects interact with the natural world of plants. Weeds growing along a street pavement often attract butterflies, as do nettles on a piece of wasteland. Allowing children time to stop as they walk along will usually provide an experience of some sort of wildlife. They may see a spider's web, a bee might fly past or a butterfly alight in a nearby garden. Adult awareness is the key to helping children develop a sense of respect and knowledge about the importance of our wildlife heritage.

In a nursery setting, space is often at a premium but this is not a barrier. Thoughtful design can provide maximum impact. Any small corner that is available can be utilized. It can be a section of a border between the boundary and the bicycle track or ball area, or you may be able to section off a small space by using some plants. Your space is three-dimensional, so look at roof space as well as floor space. Shed roofs are now becoming a focus for growing a green roof. You would need to research this and if possible, use a parent or contractor who has had previous experience. In Sheffield, there is a large primary school in the city centre that has recently developed a roof garden. Because there were no grassy areas at ground level they have used the roof, and it has been declared a 'local nature reserve' by Natural England. There is even a wildflower meadow.

It is important, as far as possible, to build into the children's everyday outdoor space, an area that is specifically designed to attract as much wildlife as possible. You will be able to maximize opportunities by using particular plants that are attractive to bees and butterflies.

It is important to include the children in the initial planning stages. Through talking to them about the importance of making provision for wildlife (e.g. all wildlife needs four things to be successful: food, water, shelter and a place to breed) you will develop their awareness and interest over a period of time.

Features of the wildlife area

Hedging

By providing a mixed hedge, no matter how small, you will be providing natural habitats for wildlife. Even a couple of metres will give shelter and food for birds if the plants are carefully chosen. Hedging plants that provide berries for birds are good, but you will need to ensure that they are not easily accessible to children. Some are very prickly too and this gives good protection for small nesting birds such as robins. Hawthorns, pyracantha and berberis are good for this. Other plants to use are beech, hazel and holly.

Walls

If you have a wall you will find that many plants will grow in the cracks, including small ferns. Spiders and bees like nooks and crannies to hide in and hollow stems left in the garden also provide winter shelter.

A pond

A pond is the most important feature of any wildlife space, but the first consideration when discussing a pond must be the safety of the children. Some settings have a pond that is fenced off, and although this is essential if it is part of the main play space, there are other ways that can give the children easier access. A safety grid or mesh can be built in as part of any new pond feature and this ensures that children can observe frogs and tadpoles for long periods of time. Staff will be relaxed and able to observe the children knowing they are safe. Pebbles set around low edges mean that frogs and newts can climb in or out. The mesh needs to be 75mm to enable access for pond creatures. Detailed advice on how to construct a pond is given in many garden books, or you can download the useful leaflet on wildlife gardening from the wildlife trust website. (See 'Further reading and useful resources' list at the end of this chapter.)

Plants to use around the edges of a pond are often referred to as marginals. Irises and kingcups provide a bright splash of colour and seem to encourage dragonflies. Children are fascinated by these whirling helicopter creatures and may well want to find out more about them.

If you decide to include a pond, please inform Ofsted about this with details of how you would ensure it was a safe area. This is in line with advice on page 34 of the Statutory Framework for the Early Years Foundation Stage.

Another project is to build a 'bug palace' and this can provide homes for many creatures and take up relatively little space.

Sensory garden

Many nursery staff will include a sensory garden in their wish list and it is again important to plan this carefully according to available space and also to consider what the benefits are for the children. Alternatively, rather than put all the plants in one specific area, if space is limited they can be planted in any part of the garden or as part of the wildlife area. Sometimes plants can be used to surround a quiet space for children to look at books, be on their own, or sit quietly with a friend. Children with sight impairment will respond to the smell and touch of these plants and a sensory garden will attract a wide range of insects and butterflies. Chapter 4, 'What should we plant in our garden?' contains more detailed suggestions.

Dens

As you discuss with the children what they would like to do in their garden, it is very likely that most will talk about having a secret space. One child said to me, as we discussed ideas for their nursery garden, 'I would like a forest, somewhere scary, but where I can hide and be safe'.

Helen Tovey (2007) cites the research by Kirby in 1989, which highlighted that richer and more meaningful dramatic play and conversation took place in spaces where children could remain hidden but see out. Dens needed to have a ceiling effect and a number of different entry and exit points. Manufactured toy play houses do not meet this requirement but a carefully planned use of bushes, bamboos or large shrubs can provide this space. Natural den spaces can be created using weeping willow or bamboo. Look carefully at any existing shrubs or trees and see if they can be used by children. A large hedge could be pruned to make a den inside it. You will need to check that any protruding branches or twigs are made safe.

A den-making kit will encourage children to think of ways to make a den. A supply of clothes pegs, rope, string, fabric sheeting and floor covering will encourage children to plan their space. Tree trunks or posts can be used to string rope and fabric across.

'If we allow children to shape their own world in childhood, they will grow up knowing and feeling that they can participate in shaping the big world tomorrow' (Sobel 2002: 161).

It is important to include some secret spaces for children somewhere in your overall design. Suitable plants and shrubs are listed in Chapter 4.

Storytelling and story-making spaces

Any quiet space can be used for storytelling, either for groups of children or for individuals to look at books. Willow structures provide secret spaces for one or two children to look at books together and larger groups can fit under a pergola. Some settings like to have a 'storyteller's chair'. This can be used by children or adults. Raised beds and appropriate planting will also create a sense of place. Think about using some evergreen plants and maybe a colour scheme. Blues and soft pinks will help to create an atmosphere of calm. Maybe a large piece of fabric can be tied between bushes or trees. You may need to insert some posts with hooks at the top to help with this.

Talking hotspots

This phrase has been used to describe a space where children feel secure and where they can engage in communication with an adult or with their peers. Small leafy spaces are ideal for this purpose and should be built in to any basic design. Even providing a large cardboard box behind a large shrub will make an ideal place for a chat.

Music area

Experimenting with sounds outdoors can be enhanced if there is a designated area. If it is enclosed, children can become totally absorbed in what they are doing without the distractions of other children at play. Planting can be used to give privacy. A small space can often be created by making an extra curve in a pathway and screening it with a raised bed and evergreen foliage. Wooden structures can be used to hang percussion instruments on and the floor space to give access to a range of different sound-making equipment. Keeping track of hand-held beaters can prove difficult and they may need to be tied to the instruments.

Ball space

Learning to control balls and other small equipment of different shapes and sizes is an important way of developing children's physical skills of balance and coordination. There needs to be somewhere they can do this, even if the space is fairly small. It may be that the space needs to be shared with different types of physical activities as children request. There may be a narrow space down the side of a building where they can kick a ball up and down to a small goal. Basketball nets at different heights offer different challenges, or throwing beanbags into hoops or crates is possible in a very small space. In a larger space, you may need to create some boundaries to prevent balls travelling long distances and disrupting other areas. Shrubs or trees can often be used to make some natural divisions.

Muddy patch

You may have a muddy patch, and if so, try to keep it, or if it is causing problems, discuss ways to make it acceptable and manageable. Children, particularly toddlers, love nothing better than to prod, poke or splash in mud. All they need is a small stick. Going for a walk on the common with my two-year-old grandson becomes impossible once he sees some mud or a puddle. He becomes totally absorbed and enters into a world of his own. This child who is never usually still for more than a minute remains transfixed often for 15 minutes or more. It may be that in your setting, the issue is suitable clothing and you will need to provide wellies and splash suits (details of clothing suppliers can be found at the end of Chapter 6). The area may need to be relocated to a different part of the garden.

Digging area

In addition to an area designated for growing plants and vegetables, it is essential to include spaces where children can dig without fear of uprooting plants. They need to be able to explore the earth and get a feel for handling tools such as trowels and forks. They need to transport earth from one place to another, so if space allows try to have two or three spaces where wheelbarrows can be taken and emptied. This will save little heaps of earth and sand appearing all over paths and paved or bark spaces. In a large space, a digging area can be a permanent feature with soil or compost and some old rotting logs to encourage mini-beasts and wildlife. Plant pots should be available for children to fill and empty. Children need to learn how to dig a hole before they can plant bulbs or plants. Learning can be enhanced by placing a box with lenses and magnifiers nearby, so children can examine mini-beasts. Reference books too need to be easily accessible.

The gravel area

Many practitioners already provide gravel as an additional medium for children's exploratory play. Often, it is in a builder's tray or a conventional plastic sand or water tray, but this can often restrict play (see case study at end of this section). If there are younger children around, raised gravel beds are the safest way to offer this material. However, if your outdoor area is accessed only by children aged three and over, another alternative way to incorporate a gravel area is to look at your overall design and discuss where you could add a small but separate ground space. Gravel fits well alongside other textured surfaces and can also be a medium for planting certain types of plants. It could be placed alongside a brick paved patio or next to paving slabs. Ideally, it should be adjacent to a hard surface rather than grass or bark as this makes sweeping up any overflow much easier and can then be managed by the children. The area can become particularly attractive with the addition of some larger boulders, securely fixed, and some plants. Hard-wearing plants that can resist a certain amount of play wear and tear, should be considered. Some of these will also provide fragrance when crushed. The area to be used should be covered with a sheet of black fleece or porous membrane and any planting done through holes in this. Larger grasses could be planted at the rear with smaller clumps where the children play. Different herbs can be planted as these will also release fragrances when crushed. Additional natural materials such as pine cones and man-made small world animals, cars or diggers will extend play. If children can access these resources independently to use in this area, it will develop their thinking skills and ensure they never become bored with the space.

Case study

On a recent visit to a school, I observed a group of five-year-old boys around a sand tray filled with gravel. They had a selection of construction vehicles, bulldozers, diggers and dumper trucks. There wasn't a lot of additional space for them to access the gravel but they managed to fill their vehicles. It was interesting to observe the development of interactive group play, as they began to fill and empty each other's vehicles and coordinate the movements. However, after about ten minutes they became bored and left the area. Close observation revealed that the play had become repetitive and there were no opportunities for them to take it further. They needed more space and maybe some open-ended resources such as guttering and planks. The teacher and I looked closely at the existing area and realized there was a wide walkway nearby. If they built a small raised bed alongside this path, made some different levels and filled it with gravel, this would give the children scope to become more involved in their play and extend their thinking. Pieces of wood, small blocks or planks nearby would enable a mass of motorways and road networks to be developed.

Rockery area

Some council playgrounds are now realizing the need for children to be given risk and challenge and have placed suitable well-chosen rocks and boulders in a group for children to climb on.

Even younger children will benefit from an area that is well thought out and will enjoy clambering on the rocks. They can be firmly fixed onto soil and a layer of mulch placed around them for all weather use. Small grasses and conifers planted in this area will give a natural feel as well as providing imaginary hiding places or food for dinosaurs. Children will have hours of fun using additional materials such as pebbles or cones together with toy animals to make a dinosaur trail, a wildlife park or a jungle.

Forest or woodland area

Although it would be wonderful for every child to have experience of native woodland and work with adults who have had forest school training, there are currently only limited opportunities for children to access this. If you have a shared space it will not be easy to develop this type of natural space. Here you will need to see if there is any woodland nearby where you can take the children. In many urban schools and nurseries there are still large areas of tarmac space or a school playing field that can be used. It is possible to create a wild woodland zone in this type of setting. Think about the best space that could be used, bearing in mind that tall trees will cast shade for much of the day. An area of around 12 square metres is big enough to make a small forest space. Around six trees can be planted around the perimeter and the floor area needs to be as natural as possible. If all existing tarmac can be removed, layers of leaf mould and bark mulch would make a sympathetic floor surface. Moss can be encouraged to grow and trees could be under-planted with native woodland plants. (See Chapter 4, 'What should we plant in our garden?' for more details.) An area like this gives a natural space where children can bring their collections of natural materials and incorporate them into their imaginative or creative play.

Slack space

This term appears in the 'Play England' booklet and is used to describe a space with no predetermined function. It may well be a woodland area, or if you have a smaller outdoor area, just a small corner that children can make their own. Additional accessible resources need to be available and children will build, create and invent. Attractive outdoor storage can be provided with baskets or large plant pots.

Sandy spaces

A sand area should be an important feature of any nursery and reception garden. One of the main advantages of outdoor play is the way it can offer a richer experience for children and sand play is an area that can be considerably broadened. At best, indoor sand play is usually offered from one or maybe two plastic sand trays. An indoor sand tray can offer children the experience of wet or dry sand; they can learn about the feel and nature of it as they pour or scoop it, pat it or fill containers. They may run cars around the sand tray or put some animals in it, but there is always the restriction of space and usually this small space is shared by four children.

If you have a shared space or need to clear everything away every day it may be that you still have to use sand trays. Try putting them outside at different heights, maybe next to a table or some low seating. This will help children to work more imaginatively as they can fill containers, or have tea parties. You may be able to combine water with sand by using a water tray or large buckets and jugs so that children can help themselves. Children will enjoy helping to clear this away at the end of a session.

If you have your own outdoor space, consider what sort of experience you would like to offer your children. You could end up with more than one sand area. Sand is such a rich and satisfying material and children can gain so many different experiences as they work with it. A child on a beach will concentrate as he builds castles, digs ditches and moats. Shells and seaweed will adorn a sandcastle or sand pies, and of course someone's toes can be buried. It is possible to recreate something of this if you offer a beach-type open sandpit, but you do need a fairly large space. If there is water nearby, and you can work out ways to combine the two, then you will be offering unrivalled opportunities for deep and satisfying play. Large rainwater tubs that children can access independently are the easiest solution. There may even be room for them to use planks and logs to build into their play design.

Young children enjoy transporting sand around, and a nearby additional smaller sand space will allow wheel barrows to be loaded and emptied without sand being spread over the rest of the garden. If you do not have space for a 'beach', think about providing a sandpit large enough for children to get in and move around. Only then can they be in control of their play and use their imagination, as the sand becomes a castle, a motorway, a car park, cakes for the oven or simply somewhere where they can wiggle their toes. You may

Figure 3.2 This sand table is in a smaller sandpit next to the main one. Children can use pulleys and gutters to create pathways and use sand in different ways.

need to consider a smaller sandpit, and there will be discussion about whether it should be covered or not. Many open spaces now offer uncovered sand. There are products designed to keep cats away, and sand keeps fresher if it is uncovered. Some sandboxes come with roofs above them. Children need to be able to get into a sandpit and it needs to be large enough to enable groups to play together. Smaller sand areas can offer different opportunities if they have wooden platforms and maybe some pulleys. Toddlers too, need to be able to sit in sand and you may need an additional smaller sandpit for younger children.

Water spaces

Again the first consideration must be the safety of the children. Discuss together the type of experience you would like to offer your children and then look at practical ways of doing this. Some settings have been able to create a natural sand and water area where there is an open sandpit with water nearby so children can use them together as on a beach. Some settings have been able to recreate a stream. This can be installed relatively easily as long as there is an electrical supply nearby for the pump. A stream can be made by choosing a strip of ground with a small slope, or if necessary, a small slope may need to be created. A reservoir is sunk at the lower end and a pump installed. The reservoir should be sealed or covered to make it safe. Piping is laid underground to the top of the stream. Black plastic is laid to form the base and covered with suitable rocks and pebbles. A switch near the pump reservoir means that staff can safely control the flow, so they are always aware when the water is flowing. Children need to learn the rules about wearing wellies, but will have endless hours of enjoyment.

If you are in a shared space it may not be possible to install features such as these. However a large tray of water or even an outside tap and different sized containers can provide endless hours of exploratory play. Children with little or no English can join in at the same level as their peers as they work out ways for water to flow at different levels using pipes and gutters.

Learning through Landscapes suggest ideas for a water-play box in their resource lists. This includes plastic jugs and funnels, lengths of hose, and gaffer tape to stick things together. Additional fun items such as a windmill, some sea creatures and pebbles could be added. A hosepipe can be used under adult supervision and children are able to water flowers and vegetables. Gutters and pipes can be used with water trays or with screens or poles. Children need to be able to move them themselves as they design new waterways. There is an article in *Without Walls* that gives details of how to make a trellis structure to hold various pipe and gutter fixings.

Many garden centres sell a variety of other water features. A small bubble fountain will give the sound of trickling water, or a covered water butt with a pump will allow children to experiment with pump suction and flow.

Walkways and pathways

As you plan your spaces, try to think of ways to connect them that will be interesting for the children and add to the learning experience. You will need to think about accessibility for all children but there can sometimes be alternative routes around stepping stones and logs. Pebbles can be cemented in to make a space safe for very young children, where they can feel the different textures. Bricks and insets on pathways make cycling more challenging and children can hear different sounds as they ride on different surfaces. Wooden walkways appeal to children from an early age as they challenge themselves to move even quicker and more confidently.

Figure 3.3 A raised bridge over a stream of pebbles invites children to explore further and go into the story tepee.

Shady spaces

Most practitioners are very aware of the need to create shade in their outdoor environment during the summer months. Many nurseries have already invested in large covered verandas for all weather and sunshades or sunsails for the summer. It is worth considering that by planting a variety of larger shrubs and trees you will be able to make natural shady spaces. Wooden or willow fencing can be used and a trellis with suitable climbers planted will also create shade. In the planting section, there are suggestions for plants that will thrive in shady areas. Willow shelters and dens will also provide shade. It might be appropriate to include a small bubble fountain or similar feature in a shady spot. The Royal Horticultural Society guides give good ideas for using pergolas in small spaces.

Sculptures

Once you have your garden in place, think about how you can enhance it with the addition of some sculptures. Photographs and models of sculptures may inspire the children to make their own. Mosaic surrounds and wall panels are easy to provide. Children will use an endless variety of natural materials to create their own works of art. Stones, pieces of wood, grasses and flower petals can be collected from different areas of a garden and if possible try to provide a specially designated area where children can make their designs and creations, so they can be left undisturbed for a period of time.

Other sculptures made of different materials may enhance the garden and provide different learning experiences. Charlie, the life-size bronze crocodile was a firm favourite at one school. He sat in among the grasses by the side of the pond area and was actually a water fountain. Children loved to sit on him and touch his scaly back. Children and parents raised money for him through a cake sale.

High spaces

Play can be transformed by height. Children are encouraged to use steps, ramps or climbing skills. Perspectives are changed and children can look down on adults. Helen Tovey writes, 'Height opens up vistas – and provides convenient vantage points for children to watch others without feeling conspicuous' (2007: 62).

Figure 3.4 This tree house was completely enclosed and a balcony made at the top with rails that were placed close together and higher than the children. It just made another special space they could use, and one where adults could not go.

A raised deck gives a wonderful feeling of space. It can be transformed into a castle, a ship, a story area or stage. Open spaces such as this encourage children and staff to work imaginatively together. Height should be designed into play areas. This can be done by building mounds and hills. High platforms can be built over sandpits.

Another way to offer height and the challenge of climbing is to use an existing tree to make a tree house. This needs to be done by experts and also the tree needs to be checked to see if it is suitable. Discuss any plans with neighbours who overlook your site.

Low spaces

If you are lucky enough to have a site on a slope, think about ways of using different levels. Initial work can be costly, but a well-planned amphitheatre or sunken space offers children a whole range of opportunity. Garden designers are including these as a feature in show gardens, but they need to be made child-friendly and on a suitable scale.

A fire pit

One of the main activities of a forest school session is building and lighting a fire with children. There are safety precautions, but practitioners are able to help children sit safely beside a fire and maybe enjoy a hot drink. Many modern children have not had this experience. Sara Knight (2009) recommends that early years practitioners should consider this activity.

> Without the experiences of safe fire, children may put themselves in danger.
> (Knight 2009: 98)

A risk assessment will need to be carried out, but it provides a wonderful learning experience. Children learn about the risks of playing with matches. They see what happens when a match is lit. They can watch the flames, feel the heat, smell the smoke and hear the crackle of burning twigs. A safe place

Figure 3.5 After the exciting sensory experience of watching the bonfire, children enjoy drawing with the charcoal.

needs to be established away from fences, overhanging trees or shrubs. Staff will need to set clear rules and boundaries for children and be sensitive to the needs of the children in the group. Children see what happens when water is put on the embers and afterwards, they will enjoy using the charcoal to draw. Parents will also need to be informed about the reasons for this activity and the necessity for safe risk-taking.

Spaces for resources

In addition to storage for children's gardening tools, bikes, prams and small games equipment, think about creating a space where you can keep the moveable resources that children need to extend their play. There may be a separate space for block storage and you will need additional storage for pipes, gutters, planks, logs, crates and tyres? You may be able to set up a creative workshop with storage systems for collections of natural materials. There needs to be a supply of glue, card and writing materials nearby.

Further reading and useful resources

Dannenmaeir, M. (2008) *A Child's Garden: 60 Ideas to Make any Garden Come Alive for Children*. Portland, OR: Timber Press. Inspirational photographs of private gardens but ideas could be adapted.

Guinness, B. (1996) *Family Gardens: How to Create Magical Spaces for All Ages*. Devon: David Charles Ltd.

Lavelle, C. and Lavelle, M. (2007) *How to Create a Wildlife Garden*. London: Lorenz Books. This is a comprehensive reference book containing all the information you need. It is designed for adults and therefore most photographs are fairly small. Children may enjoy dipping into it, but I would recommend borrowing it from your library rather than buying it for your book corner.

McHoy, P. (2001) *Instant Gardens*. London: Lorenz Books. This book has good photographs of plants and layouts for different parts of a garden. It gives ideas of details of textures and colours. The plant list contains suggestions for quick results.

Newbury, T. (2002) *Patios and Courtyards: RHS Practical Guides*. London: Dorling Kindersley.

Shackell, A., Butler, N., Doyle, P. and Ball, D. 'Design for Play: A Guide to Creating Successful Play Spaces'. Department for Education. Available online at www.teachernet.gov.uk/publications or obtainable from DfE Publications. Ref: 00631–2008DOM-EN. PO Box 5050, Sherwood Park, Annesley, Nottingham. NG15 0DJ. Tel: 0845 60 222 60. The book refers to public play spaces, but has inspiring photographs and useful advice about managing risk, and about the importance of children being able to play in a natural environment and provision for 'self-built' play.

Thomas, A. (2010) *RSPB Gardening for Wildlife*. London: A & C Black Publishers. Available online at www.wildlifetrusts.org. Download factsheet 'Gardens for Wildlife'.

Toogood, A. (2002) *Low Maintenance Gardening: RHS Practical Guides*. London: Dorling Kindersley.

Websites

Learning through 'Landscapes': www.ltl.org.uk/resources. Go to 'Find a Resource' and then click on 'Playnotes' or 'Ground notes'. Playnotes: 'The art of the sandpit' and 'Play with sand and other natural materials'. Groundnotes: November 2005, 'Good resources for outdoor play'.

www.growingschools.org.uk/casestudies. Video case study on this website, made by Coombes nursery and primary school shows children den building and also gives the rationale for including this activity in the early years curriculum.

www.routledge.com/teachers/resources/fulton. Case study from this book on building a den in a forest school setting and other case studies with ideas for spaces and managing your project.

4

What should we plant in our garden?

Introduction

This chapter gives suggestions for plants to use as you create the basic framework of your garden space.

If you have limited or shared space, you will need to choose your plants carefully, so that they meet the needs of your setting. It may be that you can only use small beds or containers. If, however, you have a permanent site, you will need to include plants in your first design plan. They will be an integral part of the space and will define the quality and the nature of experiences and play opportunities that you are able to offer your children. Structural planting can be used in a variety of ways. You may want to use plants to create dens and hidey holes. Plants can be used to define spaces, to create boundaries and contexts for play. Shade can be created by planting trees although you may need to wait a year or two for this. Scents and colours need to be considered and many plants listed in this chapter have been chosen for their ability to provide interest at different times of the year. Other plants have been listed as they are good for attracting wildlife to the garden, and some are included as they offer a variety of sensory experiences for children. You can provide a few plants in raised beds or containers to act as a backdrop to children's outdoor play or you can provide an environment that encourages children to become involved through observing and interacting. You can offer scent and colour, texture and form. Plants can also be used in play and as props for play.

Robin Moore's research cites many examples of children's use of plant parts showing significant impact on their play. 'Plants provided irresistible sensory gems, pinpoints of colour, smell and geometric forms that focused children's attention and set the wheels of their imagination in motion' (Moore 1989: 4).

He describes a child using pussy willow catkins, which they called cottontails. The children made a rabbit nest out of grass and used the pussy willow catkins as eggs: 'Father rabbit goes to look for food. We get bitty branches and make them into carrots. We know rabbits don't really lay eggs cos they are mammals. When they hatch we make boats out of leaves and sail the cottontails' (Moore 1989: 5).

Children will respond to the plants around them, but also need to experience for themselves how to prepare the soil, plant seeds and harvest flowers, fruit and vegetables. They learn about the rhythms and patterns of time as they watch a bud developing and try to guess when the flower will open, or when the potatoes will be ready to harvest.

Creating the framework

Soil types

It would be worth finding out what type of soil you have, as certain plants and vegetables will flourish only in particular types of soil. Soil testing kits can be used with older children who will enjoy mixing the soil in and watching the colours change. Most plants will grow best when the pH levels are around 6.5, but different compounds can be added to improve the balance. If your soil is heavy and difficult to work it is likely to be clay. Clematis and rhododendron will do well, but to grow vegetables you need to add lots of compost. This improves the structure of the soil, which assists with drainage as well as nourishing the plants. Alternatively talk to neighbours, have a look in any neighbouring gardens and see what is growing well. Generally speaking, the main plant groups to check are acers and azaleas. They both prefer acid soils with good drainage, but can be grown in large containers if necessary.

If you are planting a reasonably large area, I would recommend going to a good local garden centre and talking to someone about your needs. Staff are usually very helpful and some have a good knowledge of plants. Their advice is free and you may also be able to get a discount or use some of the vouchers or special offers sometimes available for schools and nurseries.

The RHS *Encyclopaedia of Plants and Flowers* (2006) gives a comprehensive guide to plants for different soil types and also lists plants suitable for different climates and positions in the garden.

Trees

Trees are often the defining feature of a garden and will be a good investment if well chosen. Planting trees is now an important part of our effort to combat climate change and global warming. There are many trees suitable for small spaces, some of which are listed below. For a more comprehensive selection you may enjoy looking at the RHS *Encyclopaedia of Plants and Flowers* (2006), which should be available in most libraries. Spring blossom and autumn colour are important features to think about as you make your choice. As trees grow bigger they provide natural shade, so bear this in mind when deciding where to plant. It is sensible to avoid trees that bear berries, as even if not poisonous they are attractive to very young children and on a windy day can fall to the ground, offering something else for an adventurous two-year-old to explore!

If you have enough space to create a woodland area, try planting some silver birch. They have beautiful white tree bark through the year and lovely drooping branches. Common silver birch varieties available are Betula jaquemontii and Betula pendula.

Other trees to consider are native trees such as oak, beech, sycamore, horse chestnut and ash, but these require more space than is usually available in most schools and nurseries. Trees bearing cones are interesting but do grow quite large, so again think of the size of your space. The RHS *Encyclopaedia* gives the full grown height and width of trees. Larch trees are attractive and unusual as they drop all their needles in autumn but retain clusters of small cones along the branches. Needles and cones both provide a useful natural play resource. They grow slowly and have wonderful bright new growth in spring.

Abies koreana (Korean fir) is very slow-growing and would be suitable in a smaller space.

Cryptomeria japonica – this group have soft foliage suitable for very young children to handle.

Cedrus deodara 'Aurea' is a slow-growing upright conifer that has lovely drooping branches of golden yellow foliage.

Dwarf conifers

These are ideal for rockery areas and need very little maintenance. They come in shades of green, blue and gold. Some low-growing junipers may grow quite large and will need some pruning. If you have a shady area, choose plants from the following groups: Abies, Taxus, Thuja and Tsuga.

Suggested varieties are:

- Pinus mugo or Pinus strobus are small growing pines, good for rockeries.
- Juniperus squamata 'Blue Star' is a flat juniper that will survive the addition of dinosaurs and small world creatures among its branches.
- Cryptomeria japonica 'Sekkan Suggi' is a golden cream colour and reaches 6 feet in about ten years.

Go to your local garden centre as they will probably have a good display and you can choose according to the space you have available.

Trees for winter interest

Evergreen conifers give a magical feel to a garden and over time will grow quite large. This must be borne in mind when planting. If there is space, consider planting a Norway spruce (Christmas tree). It could be decorated with fairy lights at Christmas and children could make decorations. These could include some seed cake balls for the birds as an additional Christmas treat.

Case study

One preschool bought young individual conifer plants from eBay before Christmas. The children decorated their own mini tree and took it home. They were ready-potted and many are still growing and will be used again next year. This unusual Christmas gift cost less than £1 per child.

Catkins appear on hazel trees in winter and the long 'lamb's tail' catkins can usually be picked in February. Corylus avellana 'Aurea' is a golden hazel with creamy yellow catkins. Salix caprea 'Pendula' is a weeping willow tree that bears enormous pussy willow catkins.

Another tree which gives interest in the winter is Salix bablonica 'Tortuosa' or dragon's claw willow – again a lovely name for children to hear. This is fast-growing and has twisted branches and shoots. It can become very large.

Spring flowering trees

Ornamental cherry trees give a wonderful display of blossom and many varieties also provide fine autumn colour. There are many varieties to choose from.

So again it is important to look at your space and find out about the size. The common varieties are less expensive than newer forms.

Prunus kikushidae 'Zakura' is an attractive weeping cherry that would also make a wonderful hidey space for children through the year.

Magnolia stellata has beautiful white flowers that appear in early spring.

Weeping silver pear Pyrus salifolia 'Pendula' is another tree whose weeping branches reach down to the ground, making a wonderful hiding space for children. It also bears creamy white flowers in the spring.

Golden larch Pseudolarix amabilis has light coloured foliage and would look good in any dark corner.

Trees for summer interest

Cornus controversa 'Variegata' is known as the wedding cake tree and has attractive green and cream foliage suitable for a medium-sized space and can be pruned to keep it fairly small.

Gleditsia 'Sunburst' is a medium-sized tree that has fern-like golden yellow foliage when young, which turns to darker green later in the summer.

Eucryphia are a group of trees that produce fragrant white flowers in the summer and Eucryphia glutinosa has glossy dark leaves that turn orange and red in the autumn.

Cercis canadensis or 'Forest Pansy' can be obtained either as a small tree or shrub. It has heart shaped leaves with shades of deep red and purple.

Another tree with beautiful deep purple foliage is the copper beech.

Fagus sylvatica 'Purple Fountain' is a weeping variety and will tolerate chalky soil.

Amelanchier canadensis 'Snowy Mespilus' has white flowers in the summer and also attractive foliage which gives good colour in the autumn.

Trees for autumn colour

The Acer family offers a wide range of trees that give spectacular autumn displays and most of them do not grow too large. Trees are commonly referred to as Japanese maples and need well-drained acid soil preferably out of winds. Young plants are not frost hardy, and for this reason you need to consider whether you can provide the right environment. If you can afford to buy a larger tree, it will have a better chance of survival and children and staff alike will enjoy wonderful colour displays in the autumn.

Figure 4.1 This used to be a bare tarmac playground. Now architectural plants and a small Acer tree make the walkway attractive throughout the year.

Common varieties are:

- Acer japonicum
- Acer Aconitifolium
- Acer palmatum.

Another popular small tree is golden false acacia or Robinia pseudoacacia 'Frisia'.

Shrubs

There are so many different shrubs available in garden centres it is difficult to know where to start. Again think of your space and consider the purpose of the plant in any specific area. It may be that you can use plants to divide your space and you will need to consider how big any particular shrub will grow. Shrubs can provide shelters and be pruned into shapes to make dens or hiding places. Evergreen shrubs will give all year round protection as well as shade and colour throughout the year.

Evergreen varieties

Abelia – can grow quite large and has attractive leaves and scented flowers that can be picked by children.

Ceanothus – good for hedging, or screening. Different varieties all bear an abundance of blue flowers according to the season. A commonly available spring flowering variety is 'Puget Blue' and a good autumn flowering variety is 'Autumnal Blue'.

Garrya elliptica – a tough leathery leafed shrub with attractive long tassels of catkins in late spring.

Choisya ternata (Mexican orange blossom) – aromatic leaves and scented white flowers in the spring. Easy to grow and maintain. The yellow variety 'Sundance' has bright yellow leaves, adding colour to any corner.

Photinia fraserii – common name red robin, an easy to grow shrub that gives bright red foliage in late spring and summer as new leaves and shoots develop. It can be easily pruned if it gets too large.

Pieris like acid soils and retain leaves through the winter. Their new leaf growth in spring is tinged with shades of orange, pink and crimson and there are many attractive varieties.

Pieris 'Forest Flame' is probably the best known. They need to be kept well watered the first year after planting but need little maintenance after that.

Viburnums are another useful group of shrubs.

Viburnum tinus 'Eve Price' has white flowers in late spring.

Viburnum bodnantentse 'Dawn' is a good shrub which will grow quite large and give lots of twiggy flowering stems that children can cut throughout the winter months.

Osmanthus delavayi can be trained to make a den and if intertwined with clematis makes an attractive space.

Shrubs for seasonal interest and colour

Spring

Twisted hazel, Corylus 'Contorta' provides interesting winter twig shapes and catkins in the spring.

Summer

Weigela are a group of shrubs that bear brightly coloured flowers to add colour to any bed.

Cornus are a group of shrubs, some of which can be pruned hard in summer to give coloured stems in the winter. Cornus alba is the most common and produces red twigs in winter when hard pruned. In the summer it has flattened heads of star-shaped creamy white flowers. Cornus 'Variegata' is a deciduous tree with layered branches and attractive pinky cream and green leaves.

Autumn

Cotinus coggyria 'Flame' – commonly known as the smoke bush. This has deep purple round leaves that change to an even deeper colour in the autumn.

Rhus typhina – commonly known as stag's horn sumach. This can get quite large and can spread by underground suckers. It has bright orange and red leaves in autumn.

Winter

Witch hazel is a good choice for any garden. The name alone merits a place in the garden as it will encourage children to sound out the rhythmic Latin name Hamamelis mollis or discuss why it might be called witch hazel. There are several varieties suitable for small spaces but these shrubs do better if sheltered from strong winds.

Hamamelis 'Pallida' – large yellow flowers in mid and late winter.

Hamamelis mollis (Chinese witch hazel). This produces bright yellow flowers with a strong fragrance on bare branches in late winter.

Climbing plants

Climbing plants create height and colour and can be planted against a wall or trellis supports to make a shelter. They are easy to maintain and often only require annual pruning to keep them in check. Clematis, honeysuckle and roses provide a mass of colour and scent in a small space.

Once established, clematis will almost look after themselves and provide a riot of colour although the flowers do not last more than a day or two when picked. When planting clematis, make sure it is planted deeper than the actual top of the plant. It is also a good idea to cut down the existing growth to about one-third. Different varieties of clematis need to be pruned at different times of the year and advice can be found on any specialist websites. However do not be put off by this. If they like the soil and conditions you give them they will continue to flower each year with very little maintenance. They can be trained through fences and trellis. Also they can be planted near existing trees and shrubs and will grow through these, making it look as though the shrub has burst into flower again. There are so many varieties it is possible to have clematis in flower almost every month of the year.

Clematis tangutica 'Bill Mackenzie' grows quickly and the yellow flowers are followed by fluffy seed heads that can be collected and used by children in their play and creative work.

Honeysuckles (Lonicera) are good plants to use. They are easy to grow, tolerant of rough treatment and give amazing scented flowers. They can be trained to form arches and shelters for the children to use. Lonicera periclymenum is early flowering while Lonicera 'Serratina' is midsummer to autumn flowering with purple and red flowers.

Roses are somehow an essential part of a garden, although the plants that grow in beds are unattractive for much of the year and not child friendly. Climbing roses, however, will provide a safe and easy way to provide the summer shower of petals for children to collect and make rose petal perfume. They add colour and scent to the garden. 'New Dawn' can be grown on a north facing wall and has pale pink flowers in late summer and autumn.

'Paul's Lemon Pillar' has pale lemon flowers in summer and for early pink flowers try 'Chaplin's Pink Champion'.

Ornamental grasses

These are becoming very popular and garden centres hold a good range to choose from. They need relatively little maintenance and can be used with good effect to make a rockery or gravel area. They need good drainage to survive the winter months. Children will enjoy interacting with them as they use play animals or figures during their small world or imaginative play. Care of grasses is easy as they just require some cutting down during the late winter, and children could help with this task. Older children will be able to use secateurs but nursery-sized scissors are often the best to use for grasses. Children will enjoy using the leaves and the flowering stems of grasses in their play and in a creative workshop, which holds a range of natural materials. Younger toddlers and babies enjoy the sensations as the grasses move against their skin and as they watch shadows and sunshine moving with them.

There are several varieties of Pennisetum, which give different effects at different heights. All bear attractive plume-like flower heads, which will appeal to children of all ages.

Pennisetum villosum is fairly small with lots of fluffy creamy white flower heads. It grows up to 60 centimetres (2 feet) and would be good in a rockery or front of a border.

Pennisetum orientale is slightly taller and has pink flower heads.

Pennisetum alopecuriades are small plants suitable for edging and the named varieties 'Little Bunny' and 'Little Honey' make them an ideal choice for a children's garden.

Deschampsia is another attractive summer to autumn flowering grass.

Stipa tenuissima is about 12 inches in height and has soft wavy fronds of silver white flowers.

Japanese blood grass Imperata cylindrica 'Rubra' has stems that turn bright red in the sun.

Ophopogon planiscapus 'Nigrescens' has deep purple leaves that turn black in full sun and can be planted in rock gardens.

Festuca 'Blue Elijah' is a good pale blue grey grass for rockeries and gravel gardens.

Bamboo

Bamboo can be planted to make screening and special den places and even very young children love to hide among it. The sound of the leaves rustling in the breeze can be heard even by very tiny babies. They will turn their heads and sometimes reach out as they respond to it. Bamboo, however, can spread quickly by its underground root system. It is a good idea to plant it in its own space where it will be suitably contained.

Perennial plants

This is the term given to plants that will die down in the winter and emerge again in the spring. A few, however, are evergreen and keep foliage for winter interest. Stachys or 'Lamb's Ears', Ajuga ('Bugle') and Heuchera have attractive leaf colours that stay on the plant for much of the year.

Salvias are a useful group of plants with many varieties of different heights but usually in shades of purple through to blue, pink and white. They are a good plant to attract insects. Salvia nemorosa 'Caradonna' reaches 75 centimetres, has deep purple flowers and is fully frost-hardy. 'Cambridge Blue' is another frost-hardy variety and has elegant pale blue flowers.

Ligularia is a plant with tall yellow spires from mid to late summer. 'Catmint' or Nepeta has spikes of purple flowers that attract the bees.

Alchemilla mollis is very easy to grow and has lots of tiny yellow green flower bracts. It could be cut frequently by children if they wanted to use it as a resource for their imaginative play. Achillea, Viola and Geum are attractive flowering plants, which could also be picked by the children.

There are so many perennials to choose from that it would be sensible to take children to a garden centre if possible, in May or early June, when many are in flower. Most can be bought in smaller containers and planted out to get larger each year. This is more cost effective, and often perennials can be split each year to give more plants either to plant or maybe even to sell. Pot-grown plants can be planted at any time of the year if they are well watered. Planting in spring, however, usually gives plants a good start and they require less care.

Annual plants

These are plants that are usually grown from seed, flower the same year and then die back. Generally speaking, growing annuals is fairly labour intensive, but some plants grow easily and quickly enough for the children to understand the process and see results. Many people buy bedding plants for containers from garden centres but they are easy to grow from seed. More details can be found in Chapter 5.

Planting for butterflies and wildlife

If you have space only for window boxes, try planting a mixture of small fragrant herbs and nectar-rich plants. Hopefully the butterflies will be able to find them and settle long enough for children to observe them. Try lavenders, marjoram, thyme and scabious.

If you can include some of the following plants in your garden, they should attract a variety of butterflies:

- Spring: primrose, rocket and aubrietia – all low-growing fairly small plants.
- Summer: lavenders, hebes, and buddleias. Buddleias (often referred to as the butterfly plant) can get quite large and need to be near the back of any border. Catmint, thyme and valerian are also attractive.

- Autumn: Michaelmas daisies. Scabious produces attractive blue flowers well into autumn and Sedum produce fleshy leaves and broad flower heads, which will attract butterflies. Sedum spectabile is the most common variety and there is an attractive red leaved form – Sedum 'Rubrum', which flowers earlier in the season.

A small clump of stinging nettles will provide food for caterpillars. Children will soon learn to respect them and also that they are needed for this purpose. There may be some conflict if you are growing vegetables (see section on cabbages, Chapter 6, page 67) as to whether you keep a food supply for caterpillars. Thistles are also good plants for wildlife as they support caterpillars as well as providing winter seed heads for birds such as finches. Teasel could be grown if you have the space. These are tall plants with spiny purple flower heads from mid-to-late summer. The flower heads also provide winter food for birds.

Planting for shady areas

Woodland zones

Snowdrops and primroses are the perfect plant for children to spot in early spring. Plants can be bought from garden centres or specialist suppliers and the common primrose is sold under the name Primula vulgaris.

The Spanish bluebell (Hyacinthoides hispanica) is an invading species so if you are planting a new area, make sure you obtain bulbs of the native English bluebell (Hyacinthoides non-scripta). Bluebells grow particularly well on chalky soil and under beech trees.

Bugle (Ajuga reptans) provides good ground cover under trees or in any shady spot.

Arisarum proboscideum is a slightly unusual plant, but its common name is the mouse plant. It has white flowers with long protruding tails, like mice, and will fascinate children. It grows well in dappled shade.

Pachysandra terminalis is an evergreen perennial with shiny green foliage, which grows well in full or partial shade in a woodland garden. It grows up to 8 inches high and needs some moisture.

Ferns

These grow well under trees as long as they get some moisture. They can be used to enhance a shady digging area. There are several common varieties easily obtained from garden centres.

Plants for other shady spots

Camellias will grow in shade and as they get larger can often provide suitable shelters and dens. Plant them where they are protected from early morning spring sunshine, to enable flowers to survive frost, as the sun causes damage if it reaches the flowers before the frost has melted.

Astrantia provide flowers that are suitable for cutting by the children, for indoor decorations or play resources. The flowers will dry easily and last well.

Bugbane grows very tall and is suitable for the back of a border or shady patch. Long stalks emerge from ferny foliage and are covered with feathery white flowers during July. Children will enjoy trying to sound out the Latin name, Cimifuga racemosa.

Hardy geraniums or cranesbills will grow easily in any type of soil and in any part of a garden. They provide good ground cover but also are tough edging plants that will survive some damage by wheeled toys and still produce bright colours for most of the growing season. Varieties that actually prefer shade are: Geranium phaeum and Geranium macrorhizum (bright pink flowers).

Commonly known as 'Lamb's Ears', Stachys byzantina is a mat-forming evergreen with grey/green leaves and pinky/purple flowers that provides good ground cover. The leaves are furry and children enjoy touching them and feeling the soft texture.

Planting for dry areas

If you are able to include a gravel bed it will be an ideal spot for some tough hard-wearing plants that can withstand dry conditions and also live alongside young children as they play.

- Armeria maritima or 'Thrift' is a strong plant that grows in low clumps and has bright pink flowers.
- Verbena bonariensis is a tall plant that will self-seed. It grows to around 3 feet so may need to be out of the way of the play space.

- Lychnis 'Jenny' has tall waving stems covered in small bright pink flowers and Lychnis 'White Robin' has white flowers.
- Gaura is a plant with small pink and white flowers borne on long stems that can grow nearly as tall as the children.
- Honesty (Lunaria annua) is a biennial plant that flowers in the first year and has attractive round penny-shaped seed heads in its second year. These can be collected by children and stored for use in creative play. Honesty will self-seed so may need to be weeded out occasionally.

Lavender grows well in dry areas and likes loose crumbly soil. There are now many varieties to choose from but the three listed are probably the most popular and easily obtainable.

- Lavender 'Hidcote' can be used for low hedging.
- Lavender 'Stoechas' has attractive flower heads with vivid purple petals emerging from the top.
- Lavender 'Nana Alba' has white flowers.

Several different varieties planted in a container or near each other make an attractive display. If the plants do well children can collect and dry the flowers and use them to make gifts, either to give to parents or sell at a fundraising event. Small lavender bags or collage bookmarks or cards are cheap and easy to make.

Herbs

These can be grown in containers or in beds but it is important to consider why you grow herbs and the best varieties to use with small children. Children will enjoy picking leaves, crushing, smelling and tasting them. Mint, thyme and sage would be suitable. If there is a kitchen on site, children will be able to grow these and take them to the catering staff to use as flavouring for sauces and meats.

Many seed companies sell herb seed collections and garden centres sell a wide range of established small plants very cheaply. If you are planting a garden, this is probably the easiest way to establish it. Basil, sage and thyme are popular. Basil will not survive a winter and needs to be re-sown each year. Mint grows quickly and can easily take over the whole area. It is better to plant it in its own container. Chives are easy to grow. They bear purple flower heads, which attract bees and other insects. Children can use scissors and cut chives to flavour salads. A small rosemary bush provides year-round foliage and attractive

Figure 4.2 An attractive wicker basket lined and with drainage holes makes a good container for a variety of herbs. It also hides an ugly drain.

grey blue flowers. It needs light pruning after it has flowered. Herbs can be grown in small pots on windowsills or in any type of containers. They can be cut frequently and used in role play maybe in a den or home corner. They can also be added to play dough to give it a different fragrance.

Santolina or cotton lavender is classed as a small shrub rather than a herb, but it is a very fragrant plant and likes warm, dry conditions so can be grown in a container or gravel bed.

Plants that should be avoided

The plants in the list below should definitely be avoided in children's spaces. In addition to these, it is worth bearing in mind there are several common varieties, which, although may not be fatal, could cause sickness if eaten; e.g. daffodil bulbs, tulips and hyacinths.

Rather than avoid these altogether, it is surely better to discuss this with children and take any necessary precautions to ensure their safety. One would not leave babies or toddlers alone with these, and if older children are planting bulbs, this should always be done under supervision. Similarly when children are planting seeds, they should always be told that seeds must not be eaten. Particular care is necessary if you are planting sweet peas, as these seeds can cause tummy upsets.

In an area that is exclusively for younger children, daffodils and tulips could be planted at the back of a border or in containers that children could see but not reach easily. Children need to understand that plants should not be eaten except those crop plants which are specifically grown for this purpose. It is important that any bulbs are stored safely out of the reach of children. Hand washing should always be a part of the routine as children come back inside.

Plants that should definitely be avoided are:

- aconitum (monkshood)
- anemones
- aquilegia
- azalea
- Daphne mezereum (berries are poisonous)
- deadly nightshade (could be found as a weed in uncleared sites)
- elderberry
- foxglove
- hellebores
- holly
- iris
- ivy
- laburnum
- lily of the valley
- lupins
- morning glory
- seeds of apple, nasturtium, sweet pea
- yew.

This is not a comprehensive list of all poisonous plants but gives the ones that are most common and often seen in gardens. I have deliberately avoided suggesting planting any shrubs and trees that bear berries. As these fall to the ground, they become immediately available to children who could quickly pick one up and swallow it without even being noticed. As they get older, children can be told not to eat any sort of berry unless it is grown specifically for this purpose; e.g. blackberry, strawberry and raspberry. Babies and toddlers, however, need a berry-free environment as they investigate and explore using their mouth. If you are unsure about anything, ask an expert for a second opinion.

Further reading and useful resources

Useful publications to buy for your pupils

As you involve the children in choosing and planting your garden, they will respond by showing an increasing interest in plants. The books suggested below will encourage them to develop this interest and in some cases explore in depth the purpose of plants in our environment and the diversity of habitats throughout the world, as well as in your own garden space.

Baines, F. (1999) *World of Plants*. London: Two-Can Publishing. An excellent book with clear appealing illustrations of everyday activities including planting sunflowers. It looks carefully at different types of seeds, roots, shoots and pollinators. There are good photographs of various habitats including woodland, rainforest deserts and ponds and a section on global food crops. It has short quiz sections and will extend children's learning about the wider environment.

Grieveson, M. (2007) *Flowers and Seeds of our World*, New York: Aladdin. A beautifully illustrated book and the clear bright photographs will appeal to children across a wide age range. There are suggestions for different activities including growing a bean in a jar. It has a good section on seeds, showing different types of seed and methods of dispersal. There are key words and a glossary of plant parts, which will appeal to the many children who love to acquire new words in their vocabulary.

Hewitt, S. (2005) *Plants*. London: Chrysalis Books, Franklin Watts. A definite one for the book box in any setting or school. It is packed with information and clear illustrations of the way different plants grow in different habitats throughout the world as well as relevant pictures of wildlife and plants around ponds and in our own gardens.

Petty, K. and Voake, C. (2007) *A Little Guide to Wild Flowers*. London: Eden Project Books, Random House.

RHS (2010) *Ready Steady Grow*. London: Dorling Kindersley. Although this is primarily aimed for parents and children it has some interesting and exciting projects. They would be ideal for childminders, particularly those who have a wider age range of children. It would also be a good book to lend to parents who wish to extend their child's interest at home

Taylor, B. (1997) *Incredible Plants*. London: Dorling Kindersley. This has vivid illustrations of different parts of plants and could be used as a starting point to encourage children's in-depth observations or to develop their creativity as they look at shape and form in the brightly coloured pictures.

Voake, C. (2009) *A Little Guide to Trees*. London: Eden Project Books, Random House. Useful reference books with line drawings and illustrations of our native wild flowers and trees.

Adult reference books and guides

Chivers, S. (2005) *Planting for Colour*. Devon: David and Charles F+W (UK) Ltd.

Edwards, J. (2002) *Plant It: A Step-by-Step Guide to Creating a Beautiful Garden*. London: Anness. This is an excellent book with easy to follow photographs on every sort of planting you would need. There are ideas for container planting as well as a comprehensive range of garden plants, and vegetables. It also has tips for aftercare and troubleshooting.

RHS (2006) *Encyclopaedia of Plants and Flowers*. London: Dorling Kindersley. This is well illustrated with useful size guides particularly for trees and shrubs.

Slatcher, J. (2002) *Gardening with Wild Plants*. Lewes, UK: GMC Publications. This is a useful guide for anyone who is enthusiastic about using as many native species as possible. There are clear photographs and a comprehensive plants lists for all areas of any garden including shade, hedges, ponds, trees and climbers. It also has details of heights of each plant and useful planting and growing tips.

Swithinbank, A. (1999) *Best Plants*. London: Harper Collins.

Titchmarsh, A. (2009) *Gardening in the Shade*. London: BBC Books, Random House.

Websites

Useful websites that give illustrations and more details are:
> www.letsgogardening.co.uk/information/poisonousplants
> www.btinternet.com/-micka.wffps/poisonous.html
> www.thekidsgarden.co.uk/poisonous-plants-faqs.html

Figure 1 A small pond can be made safe with a metal cover. Children enjoy watching frogs and tadpoles.

Figure 2 Willow screens provide shade and can be used to mark out special areas.

Figure 3 This secret den was made by pruning the inside of the large shrub (Osmanthus). Logs make small seats and tables and a clematis adds colour to the den.

Figure 4 Children enjoy making their own den in a Forest School session.

Figure 5 Children helped to plant palm trees to make a jungle pathway.

Figure 6 A 'talking hotspot'! Two large plant pots were enough to mark out this special place for a conversation. Children found their own resources from the shed.

Figure 7 These art boards are on the other side of the music area and encourage children to paint on a larger scale.

Figure 8 Large plants can be used to separate areas. This music area is a small secluded space between a pathway and a climbing space. Fixed, tuned percussion and a range of other instruments give children the opportunity to experiment with sounds.

Figure 9 Easy to set up, deck chairs, a builder's tray, water and shells provide a rich and satisfying play experience.

Figure 10 This two-year-old enjoys the challenge of balancing on a pathway in Wisley Garden. It is made of logs cut lengthways.

Figure 11 A climbing wall offers physical challenge without the need for a fixed climbing frame. Parents decorated it using shapes and colours taken from the leaves in the garden.

Figure 12 A small stream can be created with a concealed pump and pond liner on a slope. The children know they need wellies to play here.

Figure 13 The design of this nursery garden offers physical challenges to children of all ages. The small ramp is good for toddlers, and older children can balance between the poles or climb on the tree trunks and rocks.

Figure 14 Snowdrops – the first signs of spring. They can be planted in any small space.

Figure 15 Logs have been placed to make a space that children can use in many ways. Here they have chosen their own resources to 'go fishing'!

Figure 16 Children enjoy interacting with natural materials and fir cones provide interesting shapes and textures.

Figure 21 A mixture of herbs and lavenders can offer a sensory experience for children, as well as attracting a range of butterflies and insects.

Figure 22 Children become deeply involved with plants and can learn a lot about colour and pattern even in a small space.

Figure 23 Children can become engrossed when playing with natural materials.

Figure 24 As children plant strawberries they learn about the different parts of the plant.

Figure 25 Strawberry picking.

Figure 26 Eating peas straight from the pod!

Figure 27 The boys were fascinated by these pumpkins that had grown on the other side of the fence. They went on to pick them, make soup and count the seeds.

Figure 28 These two- and three-year-olds pick mint to take to the cook for their roast lamb lunch.

Figure 29 Children use watercolours as they observe and paint the daffodils in these large outdoor containers.

Figure 30 Dwarf conifers planted on a rockery make a wonderful environment for imaginative play.

Figure 31 Having resources easily available meant that this child could observe the ladybird before it flew away.

5

Growing flowers and bulbs with young children

Introduction

Growing flowers and bulbs with children is a good way to help them understand that plants are living things and, as such, should be treated with respect. They will gradually learn to care for their plants and take responsibility for them. They will observe firsthand the miracle of snowdrops in the middle of winter, and watch a tulip bud swell and open. They will watch bees and butterflies taking nectar and birds pecking at seeds. Colours and scents become important and children will be able to collect seed heads and petals to enhance their play. Suggestions of suitable plants for use in play are included in this chapter.

Growing flowers from seed

Seeds should be sown in shallow containers. March and April are the best months for sowing seeds, but you need to be able to provide some protection from cold weather and frosts. If space is limited do not plant too early. Also bear in mind that Easter holidays may affect the care you can give young seedlings and it may be better to wait until after the break.

Special seed trays can be bought but you can use recycled plastic containers as long as there is some drainage. It is worth investing in seed compost, as soil from the garden is often full of other seeds and the weeds can take over before you start. Children can fill containers with moist compost and spread the seeds thinly over the surface. Seeds should be covered with another layer of compost according to directions on the seed packet. Instructions from the seed packets could be printed out in larger print for older children to read themselves. They can help to write plant labels for these or draw small pictures to laminate and mark their trays. Cover the trays with clear polythene or cling film and leave in a warm place. Once seedlings appear, remove the polythene and keep trays damp but do not overwater. As plants become big enough, they can be planted into bigger pots or outside if there is no danger of frost. They will need to be acclimatized gradually by putting the trays outdoors by day and keeping inside at night. This process is called 'hardening off' and usually takes about a week.

Climbing plants

A useful climber to grow if you need to decorate a fence or trellis is Thunbergia alata 'Black-eyed Susan' , which can be grown from seed. It needs to be sown in March and planted out after the frosts have finished. Children can measure its growth as it twines up a trellis and produces attractive bright orange flowers, with a black centre. Sweet peas are easy to grow and each child could plant their own in a yogurt pot. Seeds germinate more quickly if they have been soaked overnight. Supervise children carefully, however, as these seeds should not be put in the mouth. Young plants should have their tips pinched out to make stronger growth when they are about six inches high (15 centimetres). They can be planted out in late April or May and need to be tied to supports. These can be canes, broom handles or special supports bought from a garden centre. Children can help to tie them in and then water regularly. Flowers need to be picked regularly and children can arrange them in vases for lunchtime tables.

Flowers for containers or beds

Nemesia will quickly fill a container and nasturtiums and marigolds are popular for their bright orange shades. Marigolds are easy to grow and will grow in dry or shady spots on poor soil. Good varieties are 'Fiesta Gitana' or 'Kablouna'. Marigolds can be planted in April or May between vegetable plants, as they help to protect the crops from greenfly and other insects that could cause damage. They also produce a natural chemical from their roots which protects against potato eel worm. Love-in-a-mist (Nigella damascena) is easy to grow and will self-seed each year. It gives blue flowers and leafy foliage that children can cut and use in their play. The attractive seed heads will also give another useful resource for imaginative and creative play.

Sunflowers

The Greek name for these plants is Helianthus – 'helios' meaning sun and 'anthos' meaning flower. There are 67 types although most children enjoy growing the very tall varieties. Many settings already plant sunflower seeds with their children. Some use it as a fundraiser, either through sponsorship or competitions to see who can grow the tallest. There are different varieties available but the most commonly grown variety for height is 'Russian Giant'. 'Moonwalker' is a variety with a yellow face and chocolate brown centre.

Seeds should be planted in April, either straight in the ground or in individual pots (newspaper pots are ideal). As they reach a height of about 3–4 inches they should be planted out, about 2 feet apart. Tall varieties will need support and are often planted next to a fence, or they can be tied to plant supports. Staking individual plants is one of the challenges of growing them. If you plant them close together to form a screen, they will support each other. You can use them to make boundaries or separate spaces for children to use in different ways. Once the flower head begins to develop, it turns to the east and children can be encouraged to find out more about this. Older children could use a compass. Once the seed heads have ripened, they can be collected and will make a good wildlife snack, or even roasted in the oven to make a snack for the children. If you can leave some seeds on the plant during the winter, it will attract birds such as goldfinches and greenfinches.

Smaller varieties suitable for window boxes and patio growing are:

- 'Music Box' and 'Teddy Bear'.
- 'Munchkin' has gold petals and a green centre.
- 'Little Dorrit' has large leaves.
- 'Pastiche' is a mixture of shades of red, buff, orange and yellow.
- 'Lemon Queen' is later flowering (September–November) so would be suitable for settings open through the year.

Wildflower seeds

If you have any spare ground or a raised bed devoted to planting flowers, try letting the children scatter wild flower seeds. These special mixes can now be bought at most garden centres and give a natural selection of plants that will attract wildlife and grow easily on any soil. It is important to remember to water in dry spells.

Bulbs

Bulbs are ideal for children to plant as they require very little aftercare. When they have finished flowering, leaves should be left on the bulb until they have turned brown. This helps the goodness to return to the bulb to encourage flowering the next year. Similarly, deadheading (removing dead flowers) prevents the bulb using energy to produce seed. Children will enjoy the task of deadheading. Plan time for children to plant the bulbs, to look at reference books, gardening books and websites to learn about what will happen to them as they grow. Spring flowering bulbs need to be planted in the autumn. Summer flowering bulbs can be planted in spring and it is very easy to use them in container planting.

Late winter and spring flowering bulbs
Snowdrops (Galanthus)

There is something magical about the appearance of early snowdrops in the winter and ideally they should be included in every garden. The bulbs are tiny and can be planted in any odd corners, round the base of a tree or along the edge of a path. They will grow under existing shrubs or in a small container. They are relatively expensive to buy from garden centres, but should increase in number each year. If you are able to cope with planting larger numbers (around a hundred bulbs or more) it is much better to buy them 'in the green'; i.e. after flowering or from a specialist supplier. These come with leaves on them and should be planted in late spring. The bulbs, however, can be planted in the autumn.

- Galanthus nivalis is the single most well-known variety.
- Galanthus 'Flore Pleno' has double flowers.

Daffodils (Narcissus)

There is a huge range of bulbs on display every autumn at every garden centre. If possible, it is a good time to take children out to choose their varieties. If you take some rulers or measures with you, they will be able to work out the sizes given on the packs and choose a range to suit your needs. Colours range from the typical bright daffodil yellow, through shades of orange, white and even pink! The smaller varieties are particularly easy to grow and can be planted in a small flowerpot or window box with good results as long as they are planted deeply enough (look at the instructions on each pack). They can be grown indoors and some varieties such as the 'paper white' narcissus are treated so they come into flower by Christmas. Mini varieties are:

- 'Tete-a-tete'
- 'Minnow'
- 'Hawaii'.

Standard sizes are:

- 'Camelot' – plain yellow
- 'Narcissus'
- 'Pheasant's eye'
- 'Thalia' white with an orange centre.

These can be bought economically in mixed bags every autumn, and are ideal for children to plant in beds or containers.

Tulips (Tulipa)

Tulips come in a range of colours, shapes and sizes, and can be used to brighten any corner. They can be planted in containers or beds during late October or November. Groups of different colours will aid colour recognition and help children to observe different shades of similar colours. They should be planted 3–5 inches deep and it doesn't even matter which way up they go in. After flowering, the flower spike should be cut at the base and leaves left on the plant until they fade and wither. This will encourage good flowering the following year.

Hyacinths

These can be planted indoors or out. They make an ideal spring bulb to grow in a confined space. Special hyacinth planters made of clear plastic or glass can be filled with water and the bulb placed on the neck of the container. It will grow without soil and children can see the roots developing and reaching down into the water. This is followed by the appearance of leaves and the flower head which will open to give an amazing perfume. Hyacinths come in shades of blue, pink and white.

Additional care, however, should be taken to ensure that children do not eat any part of the bulb and they observe hand washing routines. The bulb is toxic (see list of poisonous plants, Chapter 4, page 50).

Muscari (grape hyacinth)

These are small bulbs that will naturalize over time. If they spread and make clumps, children will enjoy picking them for flower vases. They are a clear bright blue and can be enjoyed simply for their colour. They flower from March to May.

Crocus

These can easily be planted by children in the autumn. They look well in containers and are another good bulb to grow if space is limited. There is a wide range of colours from cream through to yellows and deep purple. They are one of the earliest bulbs to flower in the year and often appear when the weather is still very cold, adding a touch of colour to any dark corner.

Summer flowering bulbs

Summer flowering bulbs need to be planted in the spring and I have listed the easiest types to grow. Others require more care and attention, but these should give good results with minimum care.

Nerines

These bulbs like a fairly light soil and do not do very well in heavy clay. They have attractive pink flowers, which will appeal to children. Nerine 'Undulata' will grow well in a dry gravel bed.

Lilies

Lilies are probably best grown in containers but could be planted successfully in raised beds. They may need to be replaced after a few years. They have a wonderful smell and will add to the sensory effects of any small space.

NB Lily beetle can be a pest as these bright red beetles will chew their way through leaves and flower buds. They need to be removed on sight and destroyed.

Alliums

There are now many varieties of this attractive onion-shaped flower. Most have purple flowers and will give shape and height to any planting scheme. They come in several different heights and this needs to be borne in mind when planting in any bed or border. If children are planting more than one type at the same time, there are great opportunities for discussion and some hands-on measuring as they decide where to put the bulbs.

Varieties are:

- Allium christophii – grows to 60 centimetres (2 feet) high and has large flower heads from June onwards; can be left in place and will self-sow.
- Allium stipitatum – another tall variety.
- Allium 'Gladiator' – grows up to 90 centimetres (3 feet) but each bulb is expensive.
- Allium oreophilum – is a short variety suitable for rockeries.

It is possible to buy mixed packs of alliums and these would be good for a dry gravel patch or wildlife area.

Agapanthus

Once planted these are reasonably reliable if given some protection from winter frosts. For this reason, it is a good idea to plant them in a pot that can be moved easily. When in pots they seem to like being a bit overcrowded and will flower more profusely. If they are planted in a border, a mulch or covering of additional compost or bark will help to protect the bulbs. The bulb will sometimes look more like a fleshy root and should be planted fairly near the surface. They give tall clusters of large round flower spikes in either white or blue from July to September.

Further reading and useful resources

Books to use with children

Carle, E. (2009) *The Tiny Seed.* London: Simon and Schuster.

Garland, S. (2004) *Eddie's Garden: How to Make Things Grow.* London: Frances Lincoln.

Godwin, S. (2007) *A Seed in Need: A First Look at the Life Cycle of a Flower.* London: Wayland.

Stewart, D., and Franklin, C. (2009) *How a Seed Grows into a Sunflower.* Brighton: Book House. The clear bright illustrations in this book will appeal to babies and toddlers and there is a sound knowledge base and information for children up to age seven. There are details of how a sunflower grows through the year and a simple experiment to do with your own sunflowers. This book will appeal to all ages (including adults).

Websites of bulb suppliers

www.jparkers.co.uk

www.ThompsonMorgan.com

www.greenfingers.com

www.nextdaybulbs.co.uk

www.qualitydaffodils.co.uk

www.gardensupplydirect.co.uk (snowdrops in the green) (need to be ordered between February and March)

All garden centres and many DIY stores will stock a wide range of bulbs.

6

Growing fruit and vegetables with young children

Introduction

Growing fruit and vegetables with very young children requires some patience and perseverance, as well as regular watering checks. However, the results outweigh any disadvantages. They will learn how to plant, tend, harvest and, above all, prepare and eat the crops they have grown themselves. Involving parents and other members of the community will help to make the job easier to manage.

A dedicated growing space is the key to success. If you are currently designing your outdoor space, think carefully about separating this space from another area, which needs to be available for children to dig freely whenever they wish. Again, the size and style of your growing area will depend on the available space. Paving slabs can be used to divide a single small raised bed into areas for different plants. Some nurseries are lucky enough to have several raised beds, while others use garden tyres, flower pots or window boxes. If outdoor access is limited, consider using plant troughs or window boxes on ledges or on the floor if you have full height windows. Growbags are useful and can be placed in special plastic trays that make it easier to water and keep the surrounding space free from soil.

What should we grow?

In this section, the crops and varieties suggested are all ones that have been used with very young children and will grow in a reasonably short space of time. If you have a very large area and adults who have time to cultivate it as well as the children, you may need to look at some of the websites or books listed at the end of this chapter for suggestions for more advanced cultivation techniques and crops.

Fruit trees

If you are able to include some fruit trees in your garden, children will be able to watch the blossom turn into fruit and then help to pick, cook and eat it. Fruit trees do not need much space and can even be grown on a wall or fence. These are called espalier or cordon trees and can grow successfully in large pots. They would, however, like all pot-grown plants, need very regular and thorough watering.

Standard trees can be directly planted in the ground. Varieties are:

- Apples: 'Bramley' (for cooking), 'James Grieve', 'Laxton's Fortune' or 'Discovery' for eating
- Pears: 'Conference', 'Doyenne du Comice', 'Concorde'
- Plums: 'Victoria', 'Marjorie's seedling', 'Jubilee'
- Peach: 'Duke of York'.

Espalier or cordon trees

Apples or pears are the most suitable fruiting tree for espaliers. These can be bought already pruned into shape and need to be trained along wires or supports as they get larger. The same varieties as listed above can also be bought as espalier trees. Before buying any of these, however, it is worth getting some advice from your local nursery if possible.

A container variety of peach is dwarf 'Bonanza'.

Strawberries

Strawberries are popular with most children and the main problem is that it is usually difficult to produce enough for everyone to taste. If you have the space, it is a good idea to use a whole bed just for the strawberry plants. It doesn't have to be more than a couple of metres in size. Lots of watering is required. You may need to put a net over the crop to protect the ripening fruit from birds, but it is very satisfying for children to be able to pick their own fruit, wash it and then eat it almost straight away. New plants should be bought from a garden centre or online supplier. They will produce 'runners' during the year, which can be cut out and planted in pots or another space to provide new plants for the following year. They can also be planted in any sort of container. Varieties are:

- Early fruiting variety 'Christine' (ready to eat in July)
- Mid-season fruiting 'Cambridge Favourite'.

Tomatoes

Tomatoes are reasonably easy to grow but again need regular attention and watering. Fruit is not usually ripe until the end of July unless grown in a green house. Young plants can be bought in a garden centre or any plant sale, but again seeds will grow easily and quickly. It is tempting to plant too many seeds, so think of your space. A grow bag will hold only three or four plants. As plants grow, they need to be supported with a cane and children can help to tie them. Any growth between the leaves and main stems needs to be pinched out to encourage fruits to form only on the main stem. This is called 'pinching out'. Varieties are:

- 'Greyhound', a pointed cherry tomato
- 'Gardener's Delight', a reliable, small, sweetly flavoured cherry tomato
- 'Alicante' and 'Money-maker' are reliable standard size tomatoes
- 'Marmande' is a larger variety with good flavour
- 'Tumbling Tom', for a container variety

Potatoes

'First early' is the term given to varieties that produce early in the year. If you have lots of space you could plant several varieties, but if space is limited try 'Charlotte'. Even putting a few sprouting potatoes in a large plant pot will give enough growth for children to discover that potatoes develop in soil. Flowers should not be picked and any small tubers or green potatoes that appear on top of the soil should be destroyed immediately, as they can be harmful if eaten. Seed potatoes can be placed in egg cartons from February onwards in a good light to encourage growth. They will begin to sprout after a few days and can then be planted to a depth of 10 centimetres with about 30 centimetres between

Figure 6.1 Potatoes planted in a jute container with handles can be moved and stored safely at the end of each session in this preschool in shared premises.

plants. They can also be grown in pots. Three large or four small potatoes should be planted about half way down the pot.

Patio growing kits usually contain five tubers of three varieties and three large planters, but are expensive, although the containers can be reused the following year. Most of the major seed companies sell these and some sell refill packs to use the following years. A small raised bed will give enough space for a packet of seed potatoes bought from a garden centre. As shoots begin to grow, earth should be carefully piled up around them. This is called 'earthing up' and encourages more side shoots to develop under the soil and consequently more potatoes!

If you have a larger area it may be worth putting down a sheet of heavy duty black plastic. Cut small holes and plant the sprouting tubers leaving a small space for water. Once the flowers have died down you will be able to pull back the plastic to reveal a crop.

Any variety will grow well, but these are the more common:

- Early crop: 'Pentland Javelin', 'Rocket', 'Charlotte'
- Main crop: 'Estima', 'Maris Peer'
- Salad: 'Nicola', 'Maris Peer', 'Charlotte'

Carrots

These can be grown successfully even in limited space. A handful of seeds sprinkled on soil in a large flower pot will give a good crop, provided it is watered regularly. Children will be able to see the orange tops growing just beneath the surface. These can be carefully pulled out as they become big enough in order to give more space to remaining plants. Carrots can be eaten raw or cooked and will grow to a reasonable size in about three months. One seed pack usually contains between 500 and 1000 seeds, so make sure the children don't tip the whole lot into the soil all at once. Varieties are:

- 'Early Nantes'
- 'Valor'.

Peas

This is another crop that is easy and quick to grow. Children can plant the seeds in individual pots or straight into the ground. If possible, soak the seeds for 24 hours before planting. This softens them and will help them germinate. It is usually more successful to plant them indoors for a few weeks and then transplant the young plants to the growing space. The tops of the plants should be pinched out to give bushy growth and the plants need to be supported with some twiggy sticks. Children enjoy helping to put these in place. The young plants need regular watering and once they have flowered, the pods start to grow and young peas develop. Children will be able to see for themselves that peas do not grow in polythene bags in the supermarket. They will enjoy helping to shell them and savour the fresh taste of a home-grown crop.

Sugar snap peas are also popular and children will enjoy the crunchy taste. These grow quickly and if planted early in the season should be ready to harvest during June. Varieties are:

- 'Onward' – this is a main crop variety and if planted indoors in March, transplanted out in April/May, should be ready by July (usually 14–16 weeks after sowing)
- 'Kelvedon Wonder'
- Sugar snap pea: 'Sugar Ann'.

Broad beans

These are easy to grow as the seeds are large enough even for toddlers to handle when planting. They can be sown in autumn or spring depending on which type you choose. I would recommend spring sowing, as children will remember better what they have planted in the space and watch the growth. A good variety to use is 'Express', which can be planted in March in most types of soil and will produce a good crop by June. Follow the planting instructions on the packet. The more pods you are able to pick, the more the plant will produce.

Runner beans

Growing runner beans with children can be very rewarding, but if you need to have crops ready before the end of the summer term, this can be more difficult. Beans are not frost hardy and cannot be planted outside reliably until the middle of May and even then some areas may get a late frost. However, if your setting is open throughout the summer or you have someone coming in to maintain the garden, runner beans are a must. They take up relatively little space and give attractive flowers early on which attract bees and ladybirds. The beans are usually prolific and can be cooked for lunch or even sold to the parents. Runner beans do not take up much ground space but require supports. They can grow over 6 feet high, so need special canes or bean poles. If you have a play area with a soil base they can even be trained up a wigwam support to make a cosy den for children to play in. Bean seeds should be planted indoors to start them off. Plastic ice cream containers will hold about six plants and need drainage holes punched in the bottom. A single bean seed can be placed in a jam jar with blotting paper or kitchen towel to hold it against the side of the jar. If the paper is kept moist children will be able to see the development of the roots and then the shoot. Recommended variety:

- 'Scarlet Emperor' – red flowers and green beans.

French beans

Dwarf French beans can be green, red, purple or yellow according to variety, and give short, bushy plants. The compact varieties suitable for planting in containers are the quickest. They usually take a couple of months from sowing to picking. If planted in March with frost protection, they will be ready to pick from June.

Compact varieties:

- 'Dual'
- 'Safari'.

Coloured varieties:

- 'Borlotto Firetongue' – red mottled
- 'Canzone' – green
- 'Purple Tepee' – purple
- 'Valdor' – yellow.

Lettuces

There are many varieties of these and you will need to consider how many you want to grow. Most seed packets contain many seeds and they need to be planted fairly thinly. Young seedlings should be planted out and children will need adult help to do this as plants are fairly delicate. Lettuces can be grown in containers such as window boxes or flower pots. Think about including some red lettuce and some curly varieties.

- A pack of mixed seeds, such as mesclun, could be used for this
- Red varieties: 'Lollo Rosso'
- Green varieties: 'Black Seed Simpson' (early harvest).

Cabbages

Cabbages need a reasonable amount of space so would not be suitable for containers but would do better in a raised bed or vegetable plot. They are not a particularly rewarding crop for very young children but you may like to try 'Greyhound', which is a pointed cabbage and crops within 25 weeks of sowing. Young cabbages will attract caterpillars and may need protection. However, children enjoy watching the caterpillars and it may be worth leaving one plant unprotected so they can observe the life cycle. Tiny yellow eggs are attached to the undersides of the leaves and hatch into tiny caterpillars, which will grow very quickly. There are many different varieties of cabbage that can be planted and harvested at various times of year and a supplier's catalogue will give detailed information.

Onions

Small onion sets can be bought from any garden centre in February onwards and should be planted out in March in a sunny spot if possible. Children will enjoy planting these as they look like tiny baby onions. It is important to help children to plant them the right way up! They need to be planted about 10 centimetres (4 inches) apart. A good exercise would be to give children an appropriately sized measuring stick to use as they plant. A small hole should be dug and the onion set placed in with the top just showing. If they are too near the surface, they may get pulled out by birds or squirrels. Even a few onions planted in any small space could be used to make a vegetable soup later in the year. Varieties are:

- 'Red Baron' for spring planting
- 'Electric' can be planted in the autumn and ready by early July.

Pumpkins

These are a fun crop but need space. They also take a while to mature and will not be ready until early autumn. They can be grown on top of a compost heap and thrive on this rich material. At one school in Berkshire where they have a lot of space, all the children grow pumpkins. They measure and weigh them and then have to work out a means of transporting them back to the classroom. This project extends the children's capacity for design technology and mathematical skills. In another nursery, the children were fascinated when the plant grew through the fence and the pumpkins appeared on the other side of the fence. They harvested them, explored the inside, made soup and even counted the seeds. Seeds need to be planted indoors and tended until they have around six leaves and are ready to be planted out. They should be stood outside in their trays for about a week first to 'harden off' before being planted in open ground.

- Variety: 'Mammoth'.

Ornamental gourds and squashes

These require similar growing conditions to pumpkins, and seeds from a mixed pack can be harvested to provide ornamental gourds for use in role play or displays, or filled with seeds to make musical instruments. Some cultures traditionally use them to make bird houses. When harvesting it is important to leave two inches of stem and make a sharp cut. This will help the drying process.

Courgettes and marrows

Courgettes can be grown easily and can even be planted on top of a compost heap. They are a useful addition to many recipes, if you are able to cook with the children. They should be planted in April, but cannot be put outside until all danger of frost has passed – usually mid-May. They need a lot of space as the plants get very big. Bright yellow flowers are formed first and the fruits soon follow. They are usually ready to pick from July onwards. They need a lot of watering. Courgettes should be picked when small. If left on the plant they get very large and taste the same as marrow. Varieties are:

- 'Green Bush' – an early maturing variety
- 'Cavili' – will produce crops without pollination and therefore a good variety for beginners
- 'Defender' – a reliable heavy cropper.

Radishes

Salad radishes are one of the quickest and easiest crops to grow and, therefore, ideal to use with children. The most common variety is red, but other colours are available if you want to experiment. Seed can be sown in a pot or bed usually during March or April. Once they show above the soil, they should be picked and eaten as they will go hard and woody if left. They start to germinate within a week of planting and are ready to harvest in about a month. They don't like hot temperatures and will quickly go to seed, so this is a good crop for early rather than late summer. Varieties are:

- 'French breakfast'
- 'Rainbow Mixed'.

Thompson and Morgan supply a pack of mixed varieties, which might appeal to children.

Mooli radishes or Asian radish

These can also be grown in the summer. Planted in May, they take about eight weeks to mature. If they are planted later in the year they can be left in the ground thorough the winter.

- 'Tsukushi Spring Cross' is winter hardy
- 'Neptune' is a white variety.

Pak choi

This is a more unusual crop to grow, but would be particularly valuable to use in settings where families come from cultures that use it in traditional dishes. Parents may be interested in helping to grow it and then helping with cookery sessions using the crops. Seeds should be raised in small pots and then planted out during May. It would be a good idea to protect plants from cabbage white butterflies by using a fine mesh net, as they will lay eggs on the plants and the caterpillars may eat the entire plant. Pak choi is shallow rooted and will grow successfully in containers. It can be grown from April to September or planted in September for a winter crop. It can be cut off rather than pulled up and new leaves will sprout from the stalk. Varieties are:

- 'Dwarf Riko'
- 'Green Boy'
- 'Canton Dwarf'.

Chinese broccoli or Kailan

Kailan is widely used in Chinese cuisine, particularly in Cantonese recipes. All the plant can be used in many dishes as well as eaten raw in salads. Seeds may need to be bought from a specialist supplier (see 'Further reading and useful resources' at the end of this chapter). Broccoli, however, takes a long time to mature and you would need plenty of space, so it can stand through the winter months. Seed should be sown directly into the ground or into pots and later transplanted from April onwards. It will be harvested late October or through the winter. It needs constant watering but once the lead stem is cut out, the plant will continue to produce more crops.

- Variety: 'Green Lance F1'.

Mizuna (Japanese greens) and mibuna

These are easy to grow and can be planted in April and harvested three to six weeks later. You can cut off individual leaves and the plants will continue to produce more. They can be grown in containers and make a feathery attractive green plant. They will tolerate cold conditions but may go to seed in very hot weather. If leaves are left for longer periods (up to eight weeks) before cutting they are sturdy enough to use in a stir fry.

Sprouting seeds

There is now a huge range of sprouting seeds available. These can be grown indoors and within a few days are ready for use in salads and stir fries. They would be excellent crops for childminders to grow indoors with children. They can be grown in trays on damp cotton wool or kitchen paper if you don't want to buy the special growing compound called vermiculite. I would suggest looking on the internet to see the available types. All the major seed companies have wide ranges of seeds and growing kits.

Microgreens

These are simply greens, salads or herbs, which are grown closely together and harvested when young. They are expensive to buy, but can easily be grown and again will provide a good indoor growing experience for children. They grow quickly and children can help to cut the leaves and prepare simple food dishes with them. Planting containers should be two inches deep and once the seed is sown they should be placed on a sunny window sill or shelf. They need regular watering.

Mushroom kits

These can be bought at any garden centre and would be particularly useful for a childminder to use or for a setting with restricted space or to pack away. All they need is a dark cupboard in the winter. They can be grown outside from spring to August. White cap button mushrooms are the most common variety.

Further reading and useful resources

Books to use with children

Cooper, E. (2009) *Growing Vegetables is Fun*. London: Dennis Publishing.

Grant, A. (2010) *Grow it: Cook it with Kids*. Basingstoke: Ryland, Peters and Small. This book is designed for parents to use with children at home, but is well organized and easy for younger children to access. There are sections on how to grow all the common vegetables and bright clear photographs of children involved in this process. Each section then gives ideas for recipes using the home grown vegetables. It would be a useful resource, particularly for childminders, as well as groups of children in nursery and school settings.

Lovejoy, S. (1999) *Roots, Shoots, Buckets & Boots: Gardening with Young Children*. New York: Workman Publishing.

RHS (2008) *Grow it, Eat it*. London: Dorling Kindersley.

RHS (2010) *Ready Steady Grow*. London: Dorling Kindersley. Imaginative recipes to use your produce, with clear photographs for children to enjoy.

Ward, S. (2010) *The Early Years Gardening Handbook*. London: Practical Preschool Books, MA Education. Lots of practical ideas for activities to involve children in gardening.

Watts, B. (2007) *Bean (Watch it Grow)*. London: Franklin Watts.

Stories to use

Jack and the Beanstalk. Traditional – many different versions available.

Briggs, R. (2003) *Jim and the Beanstalk*. London: Puffin Picture Books.

Butterworth, N. and Inkpen, M. (illus.) (2008) *Jasper's Beanstalk*. London: Hodder.

French, V. (1995) *Oliver's Vegetables*. London: Hodder Children's books.

Garland, S. (2004) *Eddie's Garden and How to Make things Grow*. London: Francis Lincoln.

Ladybird (2010) *The Enormous Turnip: Touch and Feel books*. London: Ladybird

McDermott, G. (1999) *Anansi the Spider: A Tale from Ashanti Folklore*. Washington: Turtleback.

Titherington, J. (1990) *Pumpkin, Pumpkin*. New York: Green Willow Books.

Tolstoy, A. (2004) *The Enormous Turnip*. Oxford: Oxford University Press.

Websites

www.bbc.co.uk./gardening/guides/techniques/growfruitandveg

www.dobies.co.uk

www.rhs.org.uk/schoolgardening

www.unwins.co.uk/seeds-for-kids

www.thekidsgarden.co.uk

www.thompson-morgan.com

www.allotment.org.uk

www.howtogardenguide.com

www.chinesevegetables.co.uk

www.igrowveg.com

www.gardenzone.info

www.rhs.org.uk/growyourown

www.growingschools.org.uk. Go to the early years section on this website. Download 'Get growing', 'The growing year planner' in the resource section under 'Early Years' tab; also download the fact sheet 'All about food'.

7

How do we use the garden?

Introduction

Once you begin to use any new part of your garden on a daily basis, it is important to plan for an adult to be in that space. Observe how the children use it and, if necessary, discuss appropriate ways of using the spaces. Adults too, may need support. They may feel insecure and unsure if asked to plant seeds or plants with children if they haven't done this before. It is important that adults are able to interact appropriately with children in play space. There are times when children will develop their own play and times when adult intervention and guidance can open up more challenging opportunities and extend the children's thinking and involvement. A garden is a growing living thing and as such is never completed. You will have different ideas, the children will have ideas and some of these will be inspired by the plants and spaces themselves on an ongoing basis. As plants die they will need to be replaced. A garden is an ever-changing stage set and children can help to design it. As families, staff and children begin to work together to care for the garden, there should be a shared sense of pride as well as a developing sense of contribution to the ecology of our planet.

In this chapter, there are ideas for resourcing and maintaining your spaces as well as advice on how to make the garden as environmentally friendly as possible. Finally, it looks at the issue of safety in the garden.

Organic gardening

The term 'organic gardening' is now widely used. It is worth considering, however, what this actually means and whether we can build our gardens for young children based on these principles. The main consideration is that cultivation uses manures and fertilizers derived from animal or plant remains and does not use manufactured chemical substances. When working with young children, it is obviously better to avoid chemicals, and a school garden should be risk-free in this area. The RHS gives seven policy statements on its website, but this can be summarized by saying that reduced reliance on chemicals will benefit us as it encourages wildlife and a more sustainable form of gardening.

It is now possible to buy organic seeds. This means that they have been collected from plants grown in an organic environment and free from artificial pesticides and other chemicals. At one time they were much more expensive than other seeds but now they are priced more competitively and children could be asked to decide which seeds they would like to choose.

Recycling

Composting

This is very much in line with good practice and composting is an essential part of organic gardening. In principle, most garden refuse can be recycled to produce good quality compost, which will enrich the existing soil of any garden. From the very beginning of your planning, find a suitable area where you can build a compost heap.

If you are in a shared space or have a very small outdoor area, the principles of composting can be encouraged by introducing a wormery. Special kits can be bought and although expensive, provide a fun way to teach children how worms can benefit the environment. The Wiggly Wigglers website shows a range of different designs and even has one especially for indoor use in a flat (see 'Further reading and useful resources' at the end of this chapter). They produce liquid plant food using basic kitchen waste and some very hungry worms that come with the kit.

Plastic compost bins are easily available, but not very child friendly. They are fairly high and it takes a long time for compost to rot down. If you are able to build your own bin using wooden slats or pallets, it can be lower and children can help to turn the compost and add refuse to it. In a nursery setting a small wooden box around a metre square should be big enough. If you have a spot where it can be placed on earth rather than a hard surface, this will speed up the heating and decomposition process, as worms and other creatures can pass through from the ground. If you are placing the bin under a tree or near a clump of bamboo or willow, however, put a layer of weed membrane at the bottom. This will prevent the tree sending up roots into the bin, while at the same time allowing small creatures to pass through. It is useful occasionally to turn the heap to aerate it and it also needs to be kept reasonably moist. The key to successful composting is to mix roughly one part of nitrogen rich or 'green' material with one to two parts of carbon rich or 'brown' material. Brown material can include old straw, cardboard, shredded paper, tough vegetable stems and small quantities of autumn leaves. Green materials are fruit scraps, vegetable peelings, tea bags, grass clippings, cut flowers, waste from animal hutches, and unwanted plants and soft weeds. Be careful not to add tough woody stems or any cooked food. Woody prunings should be taken to a council recycling site and it may be possible to ask a parent to help with this. Weeds need to be chopped up as much as possible before adding them to the heap.

It can take up to a year to make good rich compost for use in your garden. The process can be speeded up a little by adding an 'accelerator', which is a mix of additives and bacteria to produce specific enzymes.

Peat-free compost

Another alternative to buying compost is to use coir blocks with the children. Coir is made from dust and coconut fibres and is therefore a totally renewable product. It is shipped from Sri Lanka and because of its compressed nature costs less to import and so goes a little way to reducing the carbon footprint. These blocks can be bought from garden centres or Oxfam. Children enjoy adding water and this in itself provides a valuable learning experience (see Case study 2 on www.routledge.com/teachers/resources/fulton website).

Water

You will need access to a good supply of water if your garden is to be maintained successfully. Consider whether you can install a rain water butt from a nearby down pipe. Children will need to learn how to use this with adult help, and then should eventually take responsibility for accessing it and watering their plants independently.

There are many websites where you can buy water butts. Tesco and B&Q both give clear guides to different types, how to install them and, above

Figure 7.1 A nearby rainwater butt allows children to access rainwater easily so they can water their crops independently when the soil is dry.

all, impress the need for safety by having a childproof lid, which is securely attached at all times.

Recycling tips

If you ask children to bring in deep plastic containers and food trays they can be saved and used for planting seeds. Yogurt or small cream cartons are good for children to sow individual seeds. Many nurseries already use old CDs to act as bird scarers by suspending them over their vegetable plot. Large plastic drink bottles are cheaper than cloches and can be cut down and used to protect small seedlings from cold weather conditions. Wooden lolly/ice-cream sticks make excellent plant labels and children enjoy writing on something they have collected themselves.

Newspaper flowerpots can easily be made by the children with a little adult help and are excellent for transplanting seedlings as the roots will grow through the newspaper and the whole pot can be planted with the plant into the soil where it will decompose. Special kits are available to make the smaller pots, and larger pots can be made simply by using a long strip of newspaper

Figure 7.2 Collections of natural materials can be stored outdoors in easily accessible containers.

cut to the height of an aluminium can, rolling it round the can and tucking in the bottom ends.

Resources

As you plan your garden space, you will need to think about resources that will be needed on a daily basis and how and where to store them. Resources should be easily accessible for children outdoors. If space is limited or you need to put everything away each day, small trolleys are best. Trays can contain a range of drawing and colouring materials: pens, pencils, felt tips, etc. and different sizes of paper and card. Scissors, sellotape and glue will also encourage children to develop creative skills outside. It is important to remember that these resources need to be maintained. Pencils need to be sharpened and children need to respect where things are kept just as they would indoors.

If space allows, a creative workshop can be left outside for children to access on a daily basis. Consider stocking this with natural materials, including flower petals, seed heads, trimmings from garden shrubs, grass, catkins, tiny twigs and cones, so it offers something different from your indoor creative area.

Clipboards need to be available for children to take around the space if they want to draw plants or record growth. A book box needs to be available for children to look up names of insects and plants. Photographs and clear pictures will encourage literacy and communication skills as well as increasing knowledge and understanding.

Natural materials

If you have a natural space outside, collections of stones, fir cones, bark, etc. can be stored on this. One setting uses large stone flowerpots for fir cones and bark pieces. In a large space these can be used to make patterns or pictures on the ground. If you need to put them away each day, again they could be stored in baskets, or on a storage trolley with open access for children to help themselves. If you have a large space you may need to have more than one storage space, so children can find things easily when they need them. Moss, small sticks, seed heads, leaves and catkins stored near a den space will encourage role play.

Garden tools

Safety is again the first consideration and children need to be taught how to use tools correctly as well as how to look after them. This involves putting them away safely at the end of a session. Again, you will need to think how best to store tools in your available space. If you have a special cupboard or a tool board, tools can be matched to pictures.

Garden centres stock ranges of attractive garden tools for very young children. You may be able to get a discount particularly if you visit with the children. Small adult trowels can also be used by children aged three and older, and indoor gardening sets include tools that are small enough for toddlers to handle safely. It is important to buy sturdy, good quality tools if your budget allows.

'Yeo' mini tools are well made and can be purchased with an attractive storage bag. The children's tools by Bulldog are used by the RHS and they too are well made (see website in the 'Further reading and useful resources' section at the end of this chapter).

Wheelbarrows

These are a great item for very young children. Two-year-olds may need some initial support as they begin to work out the principles of lifting and pushing at the same time. Early learning suppliers supply plastic barrows, but it may be worth also buying metal ones for actual gardening. The plastic ones may well be used to transport all sorts of items to different places in your garden. You will need to discuss with children what can and what can't be moved.

Watering cans

You may have a hose pipe that can be used, but children love being able to fill up their own cans from a water butt, so a good selection of cans of different sizes to suit the age groups is essential.

Extras

Gardening gloves for children are also now available. Small kneeling mats might help children to focus on their work as they kneel together around a raised bed. These would also encourage any children who may not like getting dirty.

Magnifiers and insect pots

There should be a box or tray of these available outside for children to access as they need them.

Books

Think about outside storage for reference books. Laminated pictures can be left outside if you have your own space. In any shared space these need to be easy to pack away each day. Chelsea Open Air Nursery School has a supply of weatherproof information boards to leave outside and is happy to sell these. Please contact the school for details.

Clothing

'There is no such thing as bad weather – only bad clothing'. This saying is becoming more familiar, and still holds strong. Adults and children need to be suitably clothed if they are to spend much of their time outdoors. Wet-weather clothing is now accessible from many online outlets, and can also be bought from any outdoor shop.

All-in-one suits for babies and toddlers are essential if they are to explore their environment as they crawl, sit and splash through mud, puddles and wet grass. Older children can put on waterproof trousers themselves if they are large enough and a separate top should be available. Think too about the adults in your setting. It may be worth investing in some adult fleece-lined waterproof jackets. Then there is no excuse!

Figure 7.3 A log with dowel rods inserted makes an attractive and accessible storage space for wellies.

Similarly you may need to invest in some wellies! Parents may provide these but again it is important to provide suitable accessible storage. Space is often a major consideration. One school used a low window sill to put wellies on and some settings use small plastic storage green houses.

Safety in the garden

As you begin to plan your outdoor space, some adults may express concerns about whether children should be allowed to walk on logs, climb trees or balance on low walls. It is important to have a discussion about this and agree on policies. Children need to be kept safe, but at the same time they need to be able to take risks and set themselves challenges.

Walking up stairs presents a risk to a toddler, but this is something they need to learn. You will need to manage the balance between the need to offer risk and the need to keep children safe from harm. In other words, do the benefits outweigh the dangers?

The document 'Managing Risk in Play Provision: A Position Statement' (www.playengland.org.uk) states:

Children need and want to take risks when they play. Play provision aims to respond to these needs and wishes by offering children stimulating, challenging environments for exploring and developing their abilities. In doing this, play provision aims to manage the level of risk so that children are not exposed to unacceptable risks of death or serious injury.

Risk management focuses on identifying any possible hazards to children and adults, looking critically at what could go wrong and identifying strategies to deal with those risks. Environments should be constantly reappraised and necessary adjustments made (see page 21 Statutory Framework EYFS). All staff must understand that they are responsible for maintaining high standards of safety at all times. They have a duty to report anything which may cause injury and the responsible person must then act on this to do what is necessary to ensure safety of adults and children. Children also need to learn the rules for safe use of any equipment, whether it be garden tools or fixed walkways. For example, in one nursery there was a challenging walkway, but in wet weather it became very slippery so a barrier chain was put across on some days. Children learnt that they could not go on it when the chain was up, and sometimes would take responsibility themselves for putting up the chain.

By making a risk assessment for each feature of the environment that presents a possible risk, you will show that you have considered this and that additional precautions have been put into place to ensure maximum safety and minimum risk.

Most settings will have a risk assessment pro forma and guidance can be sought from your local authority. The proforma shown in Table 7.1 can be adapted to use as you wish and has been completed with reference to tree climbing as this is often an area of concern. It shows the possible hazards and precautions that have been taken to overcome them. You need to consider the likelihood of harm and the severity of harm and multiply them together to give a risk rating.

The following rating scales are usually used:

■ **Likelihood of harm**
  1. Slight – unlikely that harm will occur except in a very small minority of cases.
  2. Possible – harm may occur in some cases when exposure to the hazard occurs although there are likely to be many exceptions.
  3. Probable – harm will probably result in most cases when exposure to the hazard occurs although there may be exceptions.
  4. Certain – it is certain that harm will result whenever there is exposure to the hazard.

■ **Severity of harm**
  1. Slight – injuries are minor and can be dealt with on the premises.
  2. Minor – injuries may cause some absence.
  3. Serious – injuries though not necessarily formally classified as major may result in absence from school for more than three days.

4. Major – death or major injury is probable.

By multiplying the likelihood number with the severity number you will get a risk rating. This can then be applied using the following table:

1. Minimal – no action required.
2. Acceptable – essential monitoring should be maintained but no additional controls necessary.
3–4. Moderate risk – attention to detail is required on a regular basis.
6. Activities should not be undertaken until risk has been reduced.
9. Unacceptable – the activity should not take place until the risk has been reduced.

Ongoing maintenance

When you have been successful in establishing some or all of the features for the garden, make sure there is a framework for ongoing maintenance and care (see Table 2.2). Children should be involved as much as possible and it is therefore important that curriculum planning includes time for this. It is useful to have some interested adults who can give some additional time to overseeing the space. Parents or volunteers from the community may be happy to visit on a regular basis and assist with routine tasks of weeding, pruning and planting.

Pupils from neighbouring primary and secondary schools may be able to help as many schools are beginning to realize the importance of having a garden space.

During the winter months any ground in the growing area that is not being used can be covered with black plastic or fleece to prevent too many weeds establishing.

Conclusion

Using your garden every day will ensure that children are getting the benefits of regular fresh air and exercise. You will continue to add to it as it evolves, and as adults and children respond to the environment itself. Adults need to observe carefully the ways children use the spaces and then think creatively of ways to support children in their play.

Table 7.1 Tree climbing sample

Name of setting: _____ Risk assessment date of assessment _____

Review date _____ Activity: tree climbing

L: likelihood of harm; S: severity of harm; RR: risk rating

Possible hazard	Who might be harmed?	What have you done?	What else could you do?	Who will arrange/do this?	When will this be done?	L	S	RR
Unsafe branches	Children could fall if a branch snaps Adults could be hurt by falling branch	Tree surgeon has examined tree three months ago	Staff monitor branches on a weekly basis looking for signs of decay Tree surgeon visits annually	Team leader	Ongoing	1	1	1
High branches	Child could hit head as they climb upwards	Talked to each child about this and pointed out particular branch	Ensure children with any additional needs are supervised while climbing	Nursery assistant Mary	As children are admitted to nursery they learn rules of safe outdoor play	1	2	2
Falling from tree	Children could fall and injure body parts	Observe children as they climb Check ground under tree for any hard objects that could cause injury	Ensure staff know when it is appropriate to intervene	Nursery manager	Staff training day 'Risk and Challenge' Date TBA	1	3	3
Small twigs can be a hazard to eyes	Children by turning quickly into twig	Removed all low twigs that are in children's reach	Ensure children know about the need to concentrate as they climb	Group leaders		1	3	3

Further reading and useful resources

www.bulldoghandtools.co.uk

www.direct.tesco/buyingguides.waterbutts

www.diy.com/savewater

www.gardenorganic.org.uk. This website also gives details of useful publications. They have a series of small books on a variety of subjects for £2.59, including mini-beast identification guide, making compost and living willow. Also, a book by Sally Cunningham on growing Asian vegetables published by eco-logic.

www.handpickedcollection.com/gifts. This shows a picture of a special tool to make newspaper pots.

www.homecomposting.org.uk

www.instructables.com/how-to-make-organic-planting-pots. Easy to follow instructions but I would suggest using plastic bottles or tins.

www.organiccatalog.com

www.rhs.org.uk/organicgardening

www.wigglywigglers.co.uk

Clothing suppliers

www.puddlejumpers.co.uk

www.vikingkids.co.uk

www.waterproofworld.co.uk

Health and safety

www.hse.gov.uk

Contact

Chelsea Open Air Nursery School
51, Glebe Place
Chelsea
London SW3 5JE
Email: info@coans.rbkc.sch.uk
Tel: 0207 352 8374

8

What will we find in the garden?

Introduction

With careful and sensitive planning and planting, there is a vast array of wild-life to be discovered by children and adults. This chapter will outline the most common species in British gardens and give some further references so that you will be able to extend the children's knowledge and interests. Websites

Figure 8.1 Children find a range of small creatures in this newly made area of logs, bark and compost.

with more detail on each of the topics in this chapter are listed in the 'Further reading and useful resources' section at the end of the chapter.

Butterflies

By planting some of the species listed in the planting section you will ensure that your garden is visited by several species of butterflies and this will appeal to children from a very young age. By growing food plants they will have the chance to observe firsthand the lifecycle of the butterfly. It would be very useful to have a chart or laminated pictures of the common species so there is an instant reference guide.

It is a good idea to leave a dish of muddy water with some pebbles in it near the food plants. This provides minerals and also a dry place to land. It is also possible to attract butterflies by offering an artificial feeding station. This may be helpful where settings cannot have permanent plantings. You will need a small bowl or saucer, which can be hung up somewhere using hanging basket chains. It needs to be securely fixed with tape, blu-tack or putty. Choose brightly coloured ripe fruits. Children can cut up small pieces of apple, strawberries, bananas and oranges. Add some fresh fruit juice, ideally pineapple, as it has a strong smell to attract the butterflies. Fruit can be left out for up to three days. Alternatively soak a piece of sponge or foam in a dish with a mixture of sugar honey and fruit juice.

Birds

Even young babies will respond to the sound of birdsong and also to the sight of birds flying overhead. Older children should be encouraged to think about including suitable plants where birds can build nests. Robins in particular like bushy shrubs and hedges and are often confident enough to stay around even when children are playing. Nest boxes will also encourage birds. You could try making one or buying from a reliable source. Even if they are not used for a nest, they often provide a safe and dry place to shelter during a cold winter. Video cameras are now available to install so children can watch the process of hatching and feeding.

Feeding birds is an easy way to attract a variety of species into almost any small space. This is very important, especially during the winter and early spring. Investing in good quality feeders is important and children will soon learn to differentiate between the different types of food for different species. Unless you chose your feeders carefully you may find you are feeding the squirrels as well. It may be worth considering having one that is squirrel proof. If you have squirrels in the neighbourhood, however, children will like to watch them too.

A peanut feeder and a seed feeder are always popular with bluetits, and a Niger seed feeder will attract greenfinches and goldfinches. Insect eaters such as robins need mealworms or seed and breadcrumbs on a tray where they can safely perch. Children will enjoy making bird cake to hang out and this again is particularly important in the winter months as birds are more likely to survive a cold winter's night if they have eaten some fat during the day. It is also important to leave fresh water out for birds. Children might enjoy helping to design a suitable container. A willow screen or small playhouse can be used as a bird hide and resourced with binoculars and charts for bird identification.

Ladybirds

Ladybirds are particularly popular and children will enjoy seeing the differences in markings, maybe counting the number of spots and looking at the colours. They are very valuable in the vegetable garden as they will eat blackfly and greenfly, which can often damage crops.

Lacewings

These insects have four lacy wings and the most common variety is usually green in colour. They eat aphids and other pests and should be encouraged into the garden. Specially made bug boxes can be bought for lacewings and ladybirds but children might enjoy sticking sections of cane together and placing them near a log pile. Special attractants can be bought to encourage the insects to move in. Although lacewings are night creatures they are often seen in the day during May and August.

Bees

There are many interesting facts about bees and if children become interested in these creatures they could research some of these themselves. There are over 250 types of solitary bee in the UK, but the one most commonly seen is the bumble bee. The large queen bee and female workers have stings but the smaller male drones do not. Generally speaking bees will not sting unless they are threatened. A bee sting can often be successfully treated with a solution of bicarbonate of soda. Treatment must be in accordance with current first aid policies.

Wasps

Wasps are usually more unwelcome visitors to any garden and are attracted by fruit juices or drinks. Most people are nervous of wasps and children will quickly pick up on this fear. The best thing is to stay calm and if possible move away from the area with the wasps. They are usually seen in late summer and autumn and any rotting fruit will also attract them.

Hoverflies

Although similar in colouring to wasps, hoverflies are harmless and children would benefit from learning how to tell the difference. They have larger black eyespots and do not have the narrow constricted waist of a wasp. There are many different types of hoverflies in the UK but they all have the ability to hover above flowers and plants as they search for nectar.

Dragonflies and damselflies

If you have even a small pond or damp area you should be able to spot these fascinating creatures during the summer. Children will love watching them and finding out a bit more about them.

Hedgehogs

It is unlikely that you will see a hedgehog in the garden, but it may be that hedgehogs visit at night and children will enjoy looking for clues. There are many commercial hedgehog houses for sale but they are expensive. With support from an adult, children should be able to use the woodwork bench to design and create a home. They will enjoy finding out about hedgehogs, and may come to understand more about hibernation.

Stag beetles

Stag beetles are now an endangered species and protected under the Wildlife and Countryside Act 1981, and they are also listed as a 'priority species' in the UK government Biodiversity Action Plan. They are more common in the south of the UK and particularly around London. They develop from larva, which may take up to six years to develop. These are large white grubs with orangey brown heads about the size of an adult's little finger. They are not harmful to plants as they only eat rotting wood and should be treated with respect. Similarly, the beetles only drink juice from rotting fruit. Watching these creatures will give children endless fun as they are not as harmful as they might appear. The smaller female, however, could give a nasty nip so children need to understand that these creatures should not be handled. If you have a pile of rotting logs in a warm but not too sunny spot, you will provide the perfect habitat. There are many interesting facts about these creatures including a fascinating array of common names. They have an unusual and unique life cycle, which again would merit some in-depth study by five and six year olds. The internet has a variety of websites that give lots of information (see list at the end of this chapter).

Earthworms

'A snake, a snake!' was the nervous shout of my two-year-old grandson when he first saw earthworms in the garden. It took quite a bit of gentle persuasion to explain that this was a worm and he could safely hold it and then watch it wriggle back into the soil. Children are fascinated by earthworms and enjoy collecting them. We used to put them in large glass jars with layers of different coloured soils and sand and then cover it with leaves. This used to be a legitimate way of teaching how worms swallowed this soil and acted as beneficiaries in the garden. Now it seems rather cruel, and it is better to encourage children to put worms in a compost heap or a special wormery where they have the right conditions for their survival.

Earwigs

Earwigs may be found inside plants, in the compost pile or under logs. Their name came from the myth that they would crawl into people's ears. They have long forceps-like appendages from their rear abdomen, called cerci. They are harmless and tend to move quickly. They do not like cold weather and will dig deep into the ground in the winter.

Centipedes and millipedes

Children often find these creatures under logs and should not be encouraged to pick them up by hand. They are often grouped together and more information about them can be found on various websites, which give clear photographs to identify them. In general, the most commonly seen centipede is a gingery brown colour and has distinct antennae-like projections from its head. A millipede is usually longer and often a paler colour. Millipedes have two pairs of legs to each segment, while a centipede only has one pair.

Woodlice

Woodlice are always to be found under any log or small crevice. They actually belong to the same family as lobsters and shrimps. They have a hard shell on their back, but despite this protection they are the main food of many predators including spiders.

Snails

Although these creatures are regarded by many adult gardeners as enemy number one, children are always fascinated by them and will spend a long time watching them. They can be taught to pick them up carefully if they find one on the vegetable plot and put it in a container to place somewhere more suitable, maybe in the digging or log area.

Slugs

Most gardeners will go to great lengths to deter slugs from the gardens as they will quickly destroy young plants and vegetables. They are particularly active in damp weather. If your garden has a wildlife area and heaps of old logs it is inevitable that there will be some slugs. However, they in turn provide a good food source for some birds and hedgehogs. Organic pest control methods may need to come into force if they are a problem. Copper bands or strips are useful deterrents and a raised bed will afford more protection than open ground.

Frogs

Most children seem to know what a frog is even if they have not seen one. There has been a decrease in the numbers of ponds where frogspawn is laid and if your pond is able to attract frogs you will be well rewarded. Children will spend long periods of time observing the frogs and tadpoles. Frogspawn occurs usually in March or April and froglets are ready to emerge in June or July.

Toads

Toads are surprising creatures that can often be discovered by children when they turn over some damp wood or an old flowerpot. They have moist knobbly skins and do not live in water although they lay long strands of eggs on pondweed. These will hatch into tadpoles that look very similar to frog tadpoles.

Newts

If you build a small pond it is likely that it will become a home for newts. There are three main species in the UK and it is the smooth newt that is the most common. They will arrive at a pond during February and March ready for the main breeding season in April and May. Single eggs are laid on broad-leaved pond plants and will hatch in about three weeks. At around nine weeks the young newts, or efts, leave the pond and live on land. They are aquatic creatures with external gills, which they lose when they leave the water.

Spiders

Spiders are a source of particular interest to young children. They feature in popular nursery rhymes and children's stories. During the autumn, children will be able to go into the garden and see for themselves the amazing structures on plants and bushes as spiders make their webs, which are highlighted by tiny droplets of morning dew.

Conclusion

As a result of your initial planning you will have endless opportunities to extend children's learning as different species begin to make use of your spaces.

As well as providing magnifying glasses and bug boxes, try to provide books outside or photographs of various creatures so the children have an easy reference chart to use on the spot. By the time they have gone back to the book corner in the classroom, probably with a few diversions on the way, they will have forgotten what the creature looks like. It is important too, to teach children that they must be careful when observing creatures and they must always be returned as soon as possible to their original habitat.

Further reading and useful resources

General information: www.buglife.org.uk

Bees:

    www.hercules.users.netlink.co.uk/bee

Birds:

    www.rspb.org.uk (clear pictures and recordings of birdsong to aid identification)

Butterflies:

    www.britishbuttwerflies.co.uk

    www.kidsbutterfly.org

Centipedes and millipedes:

    www.kendall-bioresearch.co.uk

    www.animalcorner.co.uk/insects/millipedes

Dragonflies:

    www.dragonfly-days.co.uk

    www.uksafari.com/dragonflies

Earthworms:

    www.bbc.co.uk/nature/family/lumbricidae

    www.wigglywigglers.uk

Frogs:

    www.bbc.co.uk/scienceandnature/commonfrog

Hedgehogs:

    www.rons.hedgehogs.webs.com

    www.wildlife-web

    www.britishhedghogs.org.uk

    www.spikesite.co.uk

www.42explore.com/hedghog.htm (useful factsheets and activities)

Hoverflies:

www.uknature.co.uk/hoverflies

Lacewings:

www.rspb.org.uk/birdsandwildlife

Ladybirds:

www.uksafari/ladybirds.com

Newts:

www.thebhs.org

Snails:

www.kiddyhouse.com

www.thekidsgarden.co.uk/snailtrailnunt

Spiders:

www.uksafari.com/spiders

Stagbeetles

www.ptesgreatstaghunt.org

www.uksafari.com/stagbeetle

www.ypte.org.uk/animal/stagbeetle

Toads:

www.overthegardengate.net/wildlife/frogs clear pictures and facts help to distinguish between frogs, toads and newts.

Wasps:

www.keele.ac.ukuniversity.nathist/articles/wasps

Suggestions for the outdoor book box

Barker, N. (2010) *Bug Zoo.* London: Dorling Kindersley. Good for five- to six-year-olds.

Carle, E. (2002) *The Hungry Caterpillar.* London: Puffin.

DK Readers (2010) *Garden Friends.* London: Dorling Kindersley.

Kindersley, D. (2003) *Butterfly: Watch me Grow.* London: Dorling Kindersley.

Lockwood, R., Unwin, M. (illus.) and Whitley, S. (2006) *RSPB My first book of Garden Birds.* London: A. C. Black.

Magloff, L. (2003) *Frog: Watch me Grow.* London: Dorling Kindersley.

Oates, M. (2008) *All about Butterflies.* London: New Holland.

RHS (2004) *Garden Bugs Ultimate Sticker Book.* London: Dorling Kindersley.

RSPB (2005) *Garden Birds Ultimate Sticker Book.* London: Dorling Kindersley.

Stewart, M. (2008) *My Butterfly Book.* London: Collins. A board book suitable for younger children.

Unwin, M. (2008) *RSPB My First Book of Garden Bugs.* London: A. C. Black.

Unwin, M. (2009) *RSPB My First Book of Garden Wildlife*. London: A. C. Black.
These last two books contain clear illustrations and photographs suitable
for very young children. Available online from www.acblack.com

9

How can the garden support the themes and commitments of the Early Years Foundation Stage?

Introduction

This chapter shows how the development and use of your garden space can fulfil the requirements of the EYFS. It is set out under the headings of the four themes together with the principle and commitments for each. On the website at the end of the chapter there are blank action plans, which can be photocopied to support future development in each theme.

As you think about the statutory requirements of EYFS, it is important to ensure that you plan your spaces with an awareness of the needs of your present pupils in mind and also the needs of any pupils who may attend in the future. Accessibility for all children should be considered as you plan. Similarly, all parents and carers of your families should be aware of any plans for development and encouraged to contribute their own ideas. Photographs could be used to explain some concepts to families who do not speak English and all ideas should be built in at the planning stages.

1 A unique child

Principle: every child is a competent learner from birth who can be resilient, capable, confident and self-assured.

1.1 Child development

Babies and children develop in individual ways and at varying rates. Every area of development – physical, cognitive, linguistic, spiritual, social and emotional – is equally important.

Young babies will respond to the natural environment in an exciting way. They will explore sounds and sights as they see light filtering through trees, and hear rustling of leaves. Children who have physical limitations will be able to use different senses and feel a sense of calm when surrounded by plants. Children with different languages will be able to be self-assured and become involved in a deeper level of play with natural materials.

A well-planned garden provides a rich learning environment and as adults interact with children to explore and use this, all these areas of development will be covered.

1.2 Inclusive practice

The diversity of individuals and communities is valued and respected. No child or family is discriminated against.

There are many ways you can positively recognize different cultures in your garden. It may be through specific plants that will survive our climate or the addition of different artefacts, such as wooden African sculptures, Chinese wind chimes, or a Japanese water feature.

As you plan your growing season, think about whether you can include some sweet potatoes or use your vegetables to make dishes from different cultures. There are details of specific oriental vegetables in Chapter 6, 'Growing fruit and vegetables with young children'. Once you have vegetables ready to harvest, you could invite parents to come in and cook different dishes with the children. One nursery had set up a Chinese restaurant and on the day I visited they were serving noodles and stir fry made from vegetables grown in the garden. Another preschool grows vegetables and then cooks them for a special meal at the end of the summer term. They both commented on the fact that all the children seemed to eat everything.

As you plan the garden, accessibility will feature. Paths need to be wide enough for wheel chairs. This is usually recommended at around 1.5 metres.

Look critically at any climbing structures. It may be that a ramp can be added on one side or special hand rails attached.

1.3 Keeping safe

Young children are vulnerable. They develop resilience when their physical and psychological well-being is protected by adults.

Safety in the garden is a major consideration at all times. There is a need to define what could be termed over-protection for children and what constitutes a real hazard. Time will need to be spent at the beginning of your project talking through issues raised by staff and parents. Some practitioners feel children should not be given sticks and twigs. Others write about the necessity for play with natural materials. In the article, 'I made a unicorn', (download or order from www.communityplaythings.co.uk) children use sticks to represent different objects. One picks up a twig to use as a knife to cut an imaginary loaf of bread. Another responds quickly telling him he can't use that twig as it is the baby. She hands him another stick and they continue to play happily together.

Fixed climbing equipment and safety surfaces are often an easy way for staff to feel they have met the necessary health and safety requirements. However, this may compromise the level of challenge offered to children and inhibit the development of resilience and imagination. Real hazards in the garden are areas where special precautions need to be in place at all times, for example, pond areas need to be protected with grids or fencing.

Similarly a plant check needs to be made in the first instance and checked on a regular basis. (See list of poisonous plants and references in Chapter 4, 'What should we plant in our garden?')

A risk assessment should be carried out in any wild areas where there may be trees or large shrubs. Brambles may need to be cut. Nettles may be another point for discussion. Unless a child has a particular allergy, nettle stings are not life threatening. Nettles are a valuable food source for butterflies and their larvae. If a child gets stung they will learn about the plant. A dock leaf will calm and soothe the sting. Obviously large patches of nettles in an area where babies are crawling would need to be dealt with but maybe some nettles could be left in a wild patch for children to observe and learn about providing food plants for butterflies. Look critically at trees and use a qualified tree surgeon to make an additional inspection if necessary. This is money well spent.

By actively managing the risks in your outdoor space you will be able to present children with the challenges that they need in order to develop confidence and self-esteem. From a very young age, children will actively test themselves and repeat skills until they have mastered them.

1.4 Health and well-being

Children's health is an integral part of their emotional, mental, social, environmental and spiritual well-being and is supported by attention to these aspects.

Anyone observing children in a garden will quickly realize that children are generally calmer, more aware and are having fun. Enjoyment is one of the greatest contributors to mental and spiritual health and well-being. The calming and healing influence of plants and trees must not be underestimated. As a nation we are now beginning to visit gardens as a way of relaxing and finding recreation. Being outside every day is, in itself, a major contributor to physical health. Exercise and fresh air are vital for adults and children. Many children do not have a garden where they live and the nursery garden can provide physical challenge and emotional well-being for all children. Children learn to respect plants and wildlife in the garden. They learn to grow food and eating their own vegetables will encourage them to try foods they may not have eaten on a regular basis. They will learn about healthy lifestyles, the importance of exercise and fresh air as well as a healthy diet. Supportive adults will encourage them and the garden is the natural place for a young child to be.

2 Positive relationships

Principle: children learn to be strong and independent from a base of loving and secure relationships with parents and/or key person.

2.1 Respecting each other

Every interaction is based on caring professional relationships and respectful acknowledgement of the feelings of children and their families.

There are particular implications here for the way in which you approach the development of your outdoor space. It is vital that everyone is involved from the start. It is particularly important to plan time for adults to share their feelings and discuss any concerns they may have. Parents from different cultural backgrounds may not have had the experience of playing in a garden or outdoors in the British climate. They may need some time to share their own experiences and learn about the nature of outdoor play as we know it.

A shared project will enable parents to work both with their own children and the staff on an exciting new development.

2.2 Parents as partners

Parents are children's first and most enduring educators. When parents and practitioners work together in early years settings the results have a positive impact on children's developments and learning.

Developing a garden is usually a very positive way of involving parents in their children's education. Many parents are now working but if you can consider holding a garden day on a Saturday you may find that they will be able to attend with their children and also maybe help with routine maintenance or simply have quality time with their children in an open space. This is particularly important for families who are not able to access a garden of their own. Many settings are now open through the summer holidays, and even in a primary school it may be possible to open the garden with suitable adult supervision and allow families to use it. This would need to be discussed with school governors or nursery managers.

2.3 Supporting learning

Warm, trusting relationships with knowledgeable adults support children's learning more effectively than any amount of resources.

Adults must feel comfortable in the outdoor environment. If adults are involved at the initial planning stages of any development, they will be able to share concerns and overcome any issues that arise from the expectation that they will be working outdoors with young children, including babies. They have to be able to examine ways of using the environment to support learning and may need to attend training sessions on outdoor learning. By increasing their own knowledge of planting and growing they will be able to pass this on to the children. Many practitioners have had no experience of gardening and hopefully this book will help them to develop their skills and ultimately find some enjoyment in it. As one young pupil remarked, 'I just love digging'.

2.4 Key person

A key person has special responsibilities for working with a small number of children giving them the reassurance to feel safe and cared for and building relationships with their parents.

Shared experiences are the way that the key person will best develop relationships with parents and their children. The key person will become the person who best knows any particular child. Planning for appropriate learning is crucial, and it is possible to use the garden to encourage children to feel safe and cared for. Small safe outdoor spaces will help new children cope with transition. Involving parents in the garden will also help children to become involved. They could work on a new project, help to maintain existing gardens, supply plants or help with fundraising. The key person will need to ensure that they are as fully involved as possible and maybe will need to help the parents understand how much the garden space will benefit their child.

3 Enabling environments

Principle: the environment plays a key role in supporting and extending children's development and learning.

3.1 Observation, assessment and planning

Babies and young children are individuals first, each with a unique profile of abilities. Schedules and routines should flow with the child's needs. All planning starts with observing children in order to understand and consider their current interests, developments and learning.

The most important thing to consider in this fundamental statement is how to allow adults the time to observe children over a period of time and in a variety of situations. Having an outdoor garden where children become more deeply involved in their play will allow for this. It also offers a space where adults should be more relaxed and feel at ease with themselves. Ideally, the garden should be available to the children for as much time during the day as possible. Babies will often develop strategies to communicate their need to be outside, constantly turning to the door or window and even crying can denote a wish to go out. Wherever possible, toddlers and older children should be able to go outside as they wish and for many children the garden is the place they want to be. Observations of children's outdoor play can give even more information about the child's learning than indoor observations. Children are often more relaxed outside and will therefore play more freely and for longer periods of time. Watching how children use a space and talking to them about what else they would like in a space allows their interests to be extended. It is sometimes possible to leave outdoor play scenarios untouched so children can return to them the next day and continue their learning over much longer periods of time.

3.2 Supporting every child

The environment supports every child's learning through planned experiences and activities that are challenging but achievable.

Practitioners will learn to respond to the needs of the children and also be aware of the changing patterns in the outdoor environment. They will offer planting experiences at the right time of year and build in time for children to go back to observe progress and growth. They will respond to the changing patterns of weather and seasons, have appropriate resources available to make the most of a snowfall, watch melting ice and collect blossom in the spring. The key person for each child may need to make appropriate adaptations to ensure all children can join in. A child in a wheelchair may need long handled tools and a child who speaks no English may need picture cards or a good reference book to help them understand what the processes of planting are about. A supply of spare clothing suitable for all weathers should be available so that all children can have the opportunity to go outside at all times and in all weathers.

3.3 The learning environment

A rich and varied environment supports children's learning and development. It gives them the confidence to explore and learn in secure and safe, yet challenging, indoor and outdoor spaces.

Of all statements in EYFS this is the one that highlights the need for us to present something very special to our children in our outdoor as well as our indoor environment. If it is to be rich and varied, then surely it should have several spaces for various purposes and if these are surrounded by plants then they offer a richness that is far beyond anything we can create out of man-made materials. With sensitive planting, we can offer our children a woven tapestry of colour, light and sound that changes with the seasons and even the time of day. We need to consider challenge as well as safety, and think about the nature of 'risky play'. Trees, logs, sand and water can all be used to present challenge in an outdoor space as long as regular monitoring forms part of the risk management strategies of the setting.

3.4 The wider context

Working in partnership with other settings, other professionals and with individuals and groups in the community supports children's development and progress towards the outcomes of Every Child Matters: being healthy; staying safe; enjoying and achieving; making a positive contribution and economic well-being.

Anyone who has a passion for developing their practice and is looking to see how to improve their outdoor space for children will find that they become involved in the wider community. Make contact with local groups and tell them about your project. It might be possible to arrange for children to visit the local garden centre, hardware shop or library. There may be local artists or pupils from a nearby secondary school who would like to be involved. It is a good idea to visit other settings and, in some cases, you will need to work closely with other stakeholders to develop any shared space. Once you have a garden space that is working well, you will find that other practitioners will want to come to see what you have done and you will be able to share your ideas. By giving children the chance to be outside for as long as possible in a well-designed safe space that offers challenging and exciting play opportunities, as well as aesthetic and environmentally friendly surroundings, you will ensure you meet the five outcomes of Every Child Matters. Even our very young children soon develop a sense of economic well-being if they are able to grow enough vegetables to sell to their parents! By being outside for longer periods of time, and wearing suitable clothing children become healthier. Some settings have noticed that there have been less sickness absences since children started playing outside. By playing outside children become less inhibited and develop self-confidence and imagination.

Appropriate policies on safeguarding will need to be in place and this applies to outdoor spaces. Staff must be fully aware of necessary procedures and able to comply with them at all times. Similarly everyone must ensure that daily grounds and equipment checks are made where necessary and risk assessments are kept up to date.

4 Learning and development

Principle: children develop and learn in different ways and at different rates and all areas of learning and development are equally important and interconnected.

4.1 Play and exploration

Children's play reflects their wide ranging and varied interests and preoccupations. In their play children learn at their highest level. Play with peers is important for children's development.

Play is the way children learn. Through play they will develop the skills they need for later life. They will need to be creative, independent, have a sense of self-worth and be able to communicate in a manner of ways with people from many different cultures. There are many styles of play and the more time we can spend observing children at play the more we begin to understand the complexities of this process. Solitary play, group play, quiet reflective play, noisy and boisterous rough and tumble – all are part of the intrinsic pattern of a developing personality.

4.2 Active learning

Children learn best through the physical and mental challenges. Active learning involves other people, objects, ideas and events that engage and involve children for sustained periods.

Garden spaces need to planned at the outset so that they offer the physical and mental challenge both for the youngest and the oldest pupil. However, children will find ways of challenging themselves and can use materials and equipment in a way that adults had not necessarily intended or planned. Adults often need to respond to the challenges set by the children.

Children in an outdoor environment will often be able to concentrate for longer periods than indoors. It may be that in garden, children are able to leave structures overnight and thereby continue their learning the following day.

With the addition of natural materials and some other additional resources, they can extend their thinking and build on each day's learning.

4.3 Creativity and critical thinking

When children have opportunities to play with ideas in different situations and with a variety of resources, they discover connections and come to new and better understanding and ways of doing things. Adult support in this process enhances their ability to think critically and ask questions.

Even the environment itself will act as a learning resource. It is constantly changing and there are new things to discover every day. Children soon learn that if it rains, they don't need to water plants, but if it's hot and sunny they do. They learn about the life cycles of plants and animals, because they can see it for themselves and talk about it with their friends and with a supportive adult. A knowledgeable adult will help them understand the process of the rhythms and patterns of the natural world and will be able to help them find out answers through using a variety of additional resources.

Similarly, children will use the environment to enrich their play scenarios. They can turn a small space under a tree into a spaceship or a car. A small log might become the mast of a ship, leaves become food and children will use a variety of objects such as pipes, planks and gutters to explore concepts of height, weight, balance and flow.

4.4 Areas of learning and development

The Early Years Foundation Stage (EYFS) is made up of six areas of Learning and Development. All areas of Learning and Development are connected to one another and are equally important. All areas of Learning and Development are underpinned by the principles of the EYFS.

Outdoor learning is now recognized as being of equal importance to indoor learning and research has highlighted that some children learn better outdoors. Research has shown that all children, and in particular boys, will concentrate for longer periods outside. This consolidates their learning as they become more independent and show a wider use of language. As children become more involved outdoors there is often a direct effect on behaviour and less reported incidents (Bilton 2005).

The next chapter looks in more detail at each of the six areas of learning and development and suggests just a few ways in which adults can ensure that children are making progress in each area as they become involved in the garden.

Further reading and useful resources

www.routledge.com/teachers/resources/fulton/ for blank action plans.

10

How can the garden support the six areas of learning and development?

Introduction

This chapter looks at how adults can plan the use of the garden spaces to enhance and develop learning in the six areas of the curriculum. It is vital to remember that learning cannot be compartmentalized and play is an experience that encompasses learning in all its forms. Only by giving ourselves time and space to observe children at play do we fully realize the complexity of play and how it is the way in which children, from birth onwards, make sense of the world and their place in it. The EYFS requirement for each area is stated and the suggestions set out under the headings of aspects as given in 'Development matters' in the Practice Guidance for EYFS.

Personal, social and emotional development

Children must be provided with experiences and support which will help them to develop a positive sense of themselves and of others; respect for others; social skills; and a positive disposition to learn. Providers must ensure support for children's emotional well-being and help them to know themselves and what they can do.

Dispositions and attitudes

There is a requirement here to continue what seems to be a natural disposition for the very young baby, namely, their innate curiosity and ability to build on each experience to further their learning. Similarly with older children, the adults need to respond appropriately to children's observations and comments while they are outside. Concentration can be extended as children tend to work for longer periods when playing outside.

- Take babies outside at every opportunity. Respond to their interest in the sounds, sights and smells of a garden. Mobiles and wind chimes moving in the wind, dancing shadows, grasses and leaves all will help them to become interested and involved.
- Provide interesting natural objects for babies and toddlers to explore and a safe space where they can move around and explore independently.
- Provide books, photographs and websites to help children extend their interests and curiosity.

Self-confidence and self-esteem

Children can develop self-esteem outside as they set themselves challenges and then achieve them. There is more space for individual children to work at their own levels whether it be balancing on logs, climbing up a bit higher or making a piece of art work on the ground. There may be a few children who are initially uncertain about being outdoors. They need additional support from a key worker in the first instance but will usually respond quickly and positively to the spaces around them.

- Playing outdoors presents many opportunities for children to test themselves, overcome fears and inhibitions and achieve self-imposed goals: 'Look I can do it!'
- Give additional support to children who are not so confident in the garden environment until they are accustomed to using new spaces.
- Respond appropriately to children's comments and reactions. Encourage them to treat plants and animals with respect and help them to overcome any fears or concerns they may have.
- As the garden provides new experiences – snowdrops, daffodils, tadpoles, the noise of insects and birds, autumn leaves and so on – encourage children to respond to these by joining in and supporting their interest.

- Talk to children about treating the plants and animals with care and respect, and generally caring for our environment.
- Talk about similarities and differences between plants.
- Provide artefacts in your garden spaces that reflect different cultures and talk to the children about them.
- When confident with basic growing techniques try something a little different, maybe food crops from a different culture and use them in a cooking activity.
- Use the garden spaces for special events and festivals.

Making relationships

Children need to feel safe and secure. This will only come as they develop these relationships with adults and peers. Relationships are the most important single factor in enabling successful learning.

- Working and playing together in an attractive environment will help to foster good relationships between adults and children.
- Plan time to be in spaces where children can use a range of resources to create their own scenarios, joining in if appropriate, or respecting the children's wishes to play without an adult.
- Provide resources for den building so children can learn to negotiate and work together more confidently.

Behaviour and self-control

Children learn from an early age what is acceptable behaviour. Boundaries need to be set but always consider whether the boundaries are developmentally appropriate. Adults in every setting need to be consistent and it is important, right at the beginning of designing your outdoors and beginning to use it, that all adults are able to use the same boundaries.

- Work with children to agree rules and boundaries to put in place outside. Ensure any new children are aware of these.
- Use positive wording, e.g. 'please put the earth worm back in the soil', or 'keep the sand in the sand space'.
- Encourage children to use garden spaces appropriately and respect the creatures that live there.

- Having more space often diffuses tensions and involving children with additional needs in a gardening activity often helps them to concentrate on the task in hand.

Self-care

Children soon begin to learn to dress appropriately to go outside, fetching their coats and wellies in the winter, or their sun hat if it is hot. They need to learn that hand washing is important if they have been playing outside and, after initial help, will learn how to do this for themselves. A range of natural materials give children the chance to operate independently in the environment, maybe working with peers, but actually making the decisions and taking responsibility for setting out and clearing away.

- Provide a range of clothing for all weathers and ensure children are suitably dressed, talking to them about the reasons for choosing particular outfits.
- Talk about the seasons and weather and how this affects how we look after plants and also ourselves; keeping warm in winter; exercising and drinking enough water in the summer as well as using hats and sun protection outside.
- Ensure children adhere to rules of safety in the garden and observe good hygiene, e.g. hand washing, use and care of tools.

Sense of community

By working together to look after plants in their own garden, children begin to understand the concept of diversity. They learn that different plants have different needs; that they look different and grow at different rates. Conceptual thinking is encouraged as they discuss what they like to eat from the plot or help to cook different vegetables in recipes from different cultures. Parents may be able to come into school to help with cooking and use recipes from their own culture.

- Help children to use quiet spaces in the garden to develop a sense of calm.
- Growing a range of flowers and vegetables will help children to understand that they need a range of different things in addition to the basic requirements of water, soil and light. Help them to use this understanding to relate to their own needs and the needs of other children and adults in their lives.
- Plan to use the garden for music, art and stories from other cultures.
- Ensure that all families are able to visit the garden and enjoy its benefits.
- Use the garden for special celebrations and festivals.

Communication, language and literacy

Children's learning and competence in communicating, speaking and listening, being read to and beginning to read and write must be supported and extended. They must be provided with opportunity and encouragement to use their skills in a range of situations and for a range of purposes, and be supported in developing the confidence and disposition to do so.

Language for communication

Children who are given rich play experiences develop in confidence and self-esteem. They learn to talk about what they have done or what they have seen. They will listen and respond to instructions as they plant seeds and care for plants. Children with English as an additional language can feel confident in an outdoor environment as they join in on practical activities such as planting vegetables and flowers.

- Plan to provide small intimate spaces for children to use in the garden. The 'talking hotspots' will encourage conversations. Children need to feel safe and secure in order to communicate.
- Provide open-ended resources such as beams, logs, planks, cones and crates, so children will negotiate and share ideas.
- Plan your gardening activities always including new vocabulary that should be used with children. Ensure children with English as an additional language are given visual stimulus as they hear new words.
- Use correct names of plants and animals with children. Introduce Latin names as they will enjoy sounding these out.
- Talk to children as they help plant crops and listen to their conversations. Give clear instructions and encourage children to talk about what they are doing.
- As children relax they begin to communicate in many ways. Support them as they make connections or maybe make up a rhyme or song.

Language for thinking

The garden environment will give younger children the sensory experiences that they need to develop their language. As children play, they learn to negotiate and take turns. Language is part of this and as they work in the garden, they will be using words to describe what they do, what they have done or to ask questions.

- As a baby looks at various things in the garden, the key person needs to chat about the leaves moving, the birds singing or the water trickling. Babies need to hear the structure as well as the sound of the language in order to develop their thinking.
- As children make discoveries in the garden, support and develop their language by supplying more information and encouraging ideas.
- Listen to children as they are playing outside and provide resources that enable them to develop their ideas.
- Planned gardening activities will provide extensive opportunities for children to express their own ideas, ask questions and discuss what they are doing. Adults need to listen and if you don't know the answer to children's questions, make sure you know where you can find out the answers together.
- Use quiet spaces in the garden to spend time with children in sustained conversations.

Linking sounds and letters

Children need constant practice as they work in this area, and it needs to be an integral part of their daily play. Use rhymes and rhythms to provide a language-rich environment. Strings of plant names can be used with older children and younger ones will enjoy hearing simple rhymes about the garden.

- Make plant labels and sound the letters as you or the children write. A child looking at a marrow seed packet said 'That's an "M" – the same as for mummy'.
- Help children to make up simple rhymes outside, such as this one written by a four-year-old with a little help:

  Would you like to eat a bug?
  Find a spider in your mug?
  Eat your jelly from a jug?
  No thanks – I would rather have a hug.

Reading

Children need to have access to books at all times. The case study at the end of this chapter shows how children may surprise us by initiating their own learning if the resources are available.

- Plan secluded spaces where children can relax and look at books sometimes on their own or sometimes with others.
- Provide a story space in the garden, maybe with a story chair or just somewhere calm and quiet. Children can snuggle up in sleeping bags outside in winter at story time and the sense of adventure adds to their concentration and involvement.
- Provide good quality reference books about wildlife so children can access them easily as they need to use them, preferably in a box outside.
- Use books about gardening and plant life with children as you design and continue to use your garden.

Writing

Children will become involved in writing for a purpose as you involve them in the early stages of design and layout of the garden. There are then many opportunities to encourage writing, both through planned activities and children's own response to the world around them.

- Ensure children's drawings and plans are incorporated into initial designs.
- Record growth of flowers and vegetables, using photographs, drawings and script.
- Make seed packets for seed to be collected for next year, and write names on.
- Encourage children to use clipboards to draw and write about creatures they find in the garden.
- Make plant labels for all crops. These need to be weatherproof.
- Provide cameras for children to use and print pictures so they can help to write about them or use them in a book.
- Provide a range of high-quality writing resources outside so they are easily accessible.

Handwriting

The garden space is the best place to encourage early mark-making. All children can become totally absorbed as they make marks in sand, water, mud or snow. Climbing and swinging also develops the upper body movements that will help to develop the fine control needed to hold a pencil.

- Give toddlers some small sticks, and soil or mud. They will begin to make marks.
- Give children rakes to use in sand spaces or on snowy pathways.

- Provide opportunities for children to climb and hang in spaces using upper arm movements.
- Set up a creative workshop outside, provide high-quality resources and keep them well maintained.
- Provide clipboards or whiteboards that children can access and use easily in all areas of the garden.
- Allow children to make mixes with water, mud and natural materials, and then use paint brushes to 'paint' any surface they wish – maybe their den or some logs.

Problem solving, reasoning and numeracy

Children must be supported in developing their understanding of Problem Solving, Reasoning and Numeracy in a broad range of contexts in which they can explore, enjoy, learn, practise and talk about their developing understanding. They must be provided with opportunities to practise and extend their skills in these areas and to gain confidence and competence in their use.

Numbers as labels and for counting

The outdoor space often allows children to move more freely and younger children, in particular, will count as they take steps over stepping stones or climb a staircase.

Clipboards and writing materials encourage children to record in different ways. They may want to make a plan of their plot and mark in the correct number of plants. One child went round a nursery garden with a clipboard and returned with her paper full of numbers. She had copied all the price tags that had been inadvertently left on the new plants.

- Use number language all the time as you work in the garden.
- Planting large seeds, potatoes or bulbs with very young learners develops one-to-one correspondence as they learn to put one seed in each pot.
- Encourage children to work out how many potatoes are in the packet and count as they plant them.
- Assess children's learning by observing them through the year – the child who could not count to ten in February when planting may well be able to do this when he digs up the new potatoes.
- Provide numbered labels for the rows in the vegetable plot.
- Measure and record height of sunflowers in different ways.

- Grow peas and see who has the most in their pod when you shell them.
- Provide clipboards, paper and pens so children may record what they find and see in the garden.

Calculating

The garden offers a range of opportunity for calculation, as children learn to play together in the sandpit or become involved in growing and planting.

- Share out strawberries between children. 'How many each?'
- Plant potatoes – see how many are planted and ask children to count how many are left. 'How many are there altogether?' Children begin to understand rules of addition and subtraction.
- Look at rows in the garden bed or in plant trays. Three rows of six plants or maybe four rows of four pots in the seed tray may challenge children as they grasp the basic idea of multiples.
- Provide enough natural resources so children can work with larger amounts as they play, sharing out fir cones or pebbles, or small twigs for sausages in role play.
- Encourage sharing and division as they make sand 'cakes'.

Shape, space and measure

As children begin to move in different ways they respond to the spaces around them. Tunnels, arches, boxes, dens and mounds offer opportunities to explore space in many ways and at different levels.

- As you design your garden, give children basic layout plans and help them to show their ideas on it.
- Enable children to explore spaces at different levels and in different ways by providing tunnels, arches, dens, small pathways or large boxes.
- Provide resources for den building as this encourages problem solving and mathematical thinking. Children learn how to fit fabrics into spaces, use blocks or maybe twigs of similar lengths to make a roof.
- Encourage children to check plant growth regularly, maybe measuring them and talking about their finds. Use phrases such as 'taller than'.
- Provide water and containers of different sizes and shape so they can water plants and begin to understand about volume and capacity.
- Harvest the crops and sell any surplus to parents, giving children an idea of coinage and value as well as weighing or counting the vegetables to sell.

- Plan your garden to include interesting shapes, curves, rectangles, squares and circles.
- Use patterns and textures on pathways and walls.
- Go for a shape walk, but include shapes such as the spiral of a snail shell, the symmetry of butterfly wings, and leaves of different shapes and sizes.
- Provide string and marker pegs so children can mark out rows for crops, or tie string to poles to make supports for beans or sweet peas.
- Provide a wide range of assorted natural objects. Children may be able to help find some of these in the garden at different times of the year. Encourage them to create patterns and sequences using these materials.
- Encourage children's thinking by using appropriate questioning to stimulate their imagination. On finding a spider, try to avoid the very obvious closed question, 'How many legs has he got?' Instead, try, 'What do you think he eats?' or 'Where does he live?' This once led to a child designing a house for the spider and even trying to catch a fly for it. High-level problem solving came from designing the house, and fitting all the sections together, and this child, who had previously found it difficult to focus, became intensely involved with this activity.

Knowledge and understanding of the world

Children must be supported in developing the knowledge skills and understanding that help them to make sense of the world. Their learning must be supported through offering opportunities for them to use a range of tools safely; encounter creatures, people, plants and objects in their natural environments and in real-life situations; undertake practical 'experiments'; and work with a range of materials.

Exploration and investigation

Adults need to explore the garden with the children and be available to extend their natural curiosity. Plants with scents, textures and colours encourage children to use their senses and growing vegetables encourages them to taste and very often eat vegetables for the first time.

- Build walls and pathways of different materials and textures. Encourage babies and toddlers to explore these as well as older children.
- Make tunnels through plants, bamboo and willow and supply tree trunks or logs for climbing and stretching.

- Teach children about safety in the garden, how to use tools, grow food as well as flowers, and treat wildlife and plants with respect.
- Set up a nature trail; can they recognize plants using sense of smell or touch only?
- Encourage them to look under logs and stones, and provide magnifiers and reference books to extend their learning.
- Observe changing patterns through the day and through the seasons.
- Stimulate discussion by measuring shadow patterns on the ground and give children a sense of how our world works.
- Encourage questions and discussion with phrases like, 'What makes seeds grow?', 'Why do some trees lose their leaves and not others?' or 'Why do leaves change colour?'
- Recognize that children can use the garden to begin to understand processes of death and decay as well as growth and new life. Adults need to respond to questions and provoke thoughtful discussion.

Designing and making

Children need a wide range of easily accessible resources and spaces set aside so they can work to develop their own ideas.

- Provide blocks of wood, small and large, and a space for children to use them as they wish. They may use them together with sand and water, building car parks or castles.
- Encourage children to collect materials from the environment and use them in their play.
- Involve children in the design and construction of your garden.
- They can help put together a raised bed or lay cobbles in patterns for a pathway.

ICT

Learning in the garden can be supported in a number of ways using technology. The internet gives a range of information about wildlife and plants, while digital cameras can be used to record garden development and also growth of plants over time.

- Include an electrical socket outside where children can use tape recorders.
- Provide a digital camera for children to use. This will support learning in all areas of the curriculum. It can be used to record growth of plants and

crops. When printed out, the pictures provide a record for children to use as they look back and see how plants grow over time and how the seasons affect the lifecycles.

- Consider using safe internet sites with children. Parental permission should be gained. The Royal Society for the Protection of Birds (RSPB) has a site where children can listen to birdsong and learn to recognize different calls.
- Buy a nest box camera for use in your bird box. Children will learn how the picture on the screen links to the activity as it is taking place in the box.

Time

Developing a garden project over time and involving children from the start gives first-hand experience of time as does growing their own crops.

- Keep photographic records of planting crops and use these with children over time, so they are able to recall previous experiences. 'Do you remember planting these bulbs in September? The buds are just showing now.' 'You look smaller in these pictures. I think you have grown too!'
- Use language of time as you discuss growth of plants and trees. Some grow quickly and some more slowly, taking years to reach maturity.

Place

Children seem to have an innate sense of space. One setting discovered that children talked about the spaces in their outdoor area as places using prepositions to describe where they liked to be, e.g. 'behind the shed'.

- Observe the ways children use your outdoor space and use the information to plan your new garden.
- Plan spaces or places with definite focus so children respond appropriately.
- Make a 'wildlife space' with suitable plants, a small pond and some seating to allow adults and children to observe a variety of wildlife.
- Arrange to visit a local garden centre if possible or a shop to buy resources for your garden. Go to the local park or community space and discuss with children whether there are ideas you can use in your garden.

Community

As children become confident and secure within the community of the nursery they are able to develop awareness of other cultures and the immediate community where they live. A garden offers many opportunities to support this.

- As you gain in confidence, try planting vegetables and plants from different cultures.
- Plan cooking activities to use your crops – maybe soup or a Chinese stir fry.
- Make a storytelling space in the garden and decorate it with artefacts from other cultures.
- Invite a visiting artist or musician to work with children in the garden.
- Encourage all your parents and families to visit and use the garden when possible.
- Use the garden to celebrate festivals. Diwali lights can be placed around it and you can decorate trees at Christmas. Hold a carnival and process around the garden. Similarly, celebrate Chinese New Year with a procession and help children make an exciting trail of pathways around plants decorated with paper lanterns.

Physical development

The physical development of babies and young children must be encouraged through the provision of opportunities for them to be active and interactive and to improve their skills of coordination, control, manipulation and movement. They must be supported in using all of their senses to learn about the world around them and to make connections between new information and what they already know. They must be supported in developing an understanding of the importance of physical activity and making healthy choices in relation to food.

Movement and space

Young babies from the age of six months enter a stage where physical development becomes increasingly important as they progress from lying to sitting and crawling to walking. Outside space will enable them to move more freely than in a room and consequently they can develop confidence by going further distances and meeting more challenges. Older children need to be physically challenged as they have so much energy and need to exercise all parts of their bodies.

- Ensure the space is safe for babies, as they tend to put things in their mouths. Provide crawling areas with grass, moss and leaves.
- Design pathways of various textures, low ramps and walkways surrounded with plants and moving grasses.

- Use plants with a variety of colours, smells and textures to stimulate children's awareness of sensory experience.
- If you have trees, can they be safely used for climbing or for a tree house with ladders?
- Encourage children to watch leaves and branches moving and suggest that they can move in different ways, swaying and bending like the branches.
- Provide climbing opportunities with planks and beams, logs and stepping stones. Think of ways these can be moved around your space to provide different challenges and opportunities to develop movement of different body parts.
- Children need space for running so if possible plan your garden with small pathways wide enough for wheelchair users and wheeled toys to pass each other.

Health and body awareness

A well-planned garden can offer opportunities for healthy physical activity as well as places where plants are used to create a sense of calm and relaxation.

- Work with children to grow their own food and plan activities to use the food when it is ready to harvest.
- Give children the chance to observe growth of plants and process information about lifecycles of plants and animals in the garden.
- Discuss the merits of eating fresh fruit and vegetables as opposed to biscuits, sweets and fried food.
- Give children as much time outside as possible regardless of weather conditions. Fresh air and rain is healthy if children and adults are suitably dressed and going out in the rain is exciting for young children as they taste raindrops, run, jump and splash in puddles.
- Provide suitable storage for outdoor clothing and footwear.
- Provide special places for babies to sleep outside, perhaps under a tree.
- Provide quiet spaces where children can be relaxed and calm.
- Talk about the way they are using their muscles. Observe wild creatures and encourage children to move like a frog, a snail or a butterfly.
- Ensure there is a supply of drinking water outside and encourage children to use it, especially if the weather is hot.
- Ask children to feel their heartbeats before and after more strenuous physical activity. Discuss why exercise is part of a healthy lifestyle.
- Encourage good hygiene habits. Plants also get diseased if not given the

right growing conditions. Children can help wash plant pots and clean tools. Then they must wash their own hands.

Using equipment and materials

Children need to explore sand and water on as large a scale as possible. They will progress from exploring with twigs and sticks to using tools designed for specific purposes. A wide range of man-made and natural materials should be provided with appropriate storage.

- Provide a range of large and small equipment for children to hit, throw and catch. Plan a space for this into your garden design.
- Use a range of natural materials. Smooth pebbles and fir cones will stimulate a baby's curiosity and they will develop fine motor skills as they try to pick them up.
- Planting seeds, collecting conkers, acorns and fir cones, and cutting and arranging flowers all help to develop fine motor skills.
- Help children to tie string to bean poles and transplant seedlings.
- Provide a separate digging area. Children need to scratch around, look for mini-beasts and explore the properties of soil. Keep it moist and top up with compost if it gets too dry.
- Ensure each child learns how to use tools safely and encourage them to put tools away and care for them.
- Provide a separate planting and growing space and have separate tools for use in this area. They could be larger and need to be used for specific purposes (e.g. a rake, hoe or long-handled fork). Children must learn the rules for safe handling of these tools.
- Sand and water are basic elements and using these gives a wide range of opportunities for using different equipment. Watering plants, using a hose or a watering can, and mixing water and coir all need a reasonable degree of skill, which will only develop with practise.

Creative development

Children's creativity must be extended by the provision of support for their curiosity, exploration and play. They must be provided with opportunities to explore and share their thoughts, ideas and feelings, for example, through a variety of art, music, movement, dance, imaginative and role-play activities, mathematics, and design and technology.

Responding to experiences, expressing and communicating ideas

A garden will provide a wealth of experiences to stimulate children's curiosity, but it needs the interest and involvement of adults who are also excited by the same things as the children and willing to embark on a journey of discovery together.

- Make spaces where children can develop their imagination; a large platform, maybe at a different level, can become a ship, a stage or a castle. Dense bushes make exciting places to hide.
- Plant a wide range of plants with colour, scent and texture and make time to observe them with children.
- A wildlife garden is the source of different sights and sounds at various times of year and children will respond to these in different ways.
- Seasonal changes need to be observed and children can be outside catching raindrops, leaves or snowflakes. Children may respond by moving like the snowflakes or trees in the wind and making up songs and rhymes.

Exploring media and materials

As children observe the changes in plants and seasons they need high-quality materials and adult encouragement to allow them to respond creatively.

- Use plants that give seasonal interest and encourage children to observe the changing colours.
- Provide high-quality materials that can be accessed easily by children.
- Use a wide range of different media, not just felt pens and crayons. Offer crayons in a range of shades of greens or yellows as children draw daffodils, or white chalks, fine brushes and white and green paint when the snowdrops appear.
- Plan spaces for art boards outside, but also small spaces with comfortable seating and a supply of clipboards.
- Set up a creative workshop area outside where children can access a range of natural materials and use with card, paper, glue and scissors. Include small trimmings from plants and shrubs, grasses, petals, catkins, leaves and stems.
- Have a good supply of natural materials that children can access and use in play. Offer fir cones, moss, conkers, chestnuts and spiky cases, shells, pebbles, bark, grasses, leaves and twigs. If possible make a designated space, where children can lay these out on the ground to make patterns or create pictures

and sculptures. You may also need to provide an additional storage place for resources to be used in role play.

Creating music and dance

Special places can be planned where children can experiment freely with a range of sounds. A small stage made from blocks may encourage dance, but children may be stimulated to move spontaneously in any area of a garden.

- Develop listening awareness by taking babies outside regularly and in different weather conditions.
- Provide a safe installation of trickling water.
- Use plants with rustling leaves and encourage birds to visit the garden.
- Add wind chimes, metal and wooden, with different pitches.
- Use plants to surround a space where you can hang a range of musical instruments for children to use freely.
- Provide tape recorders for children to record sounds and songs outside.
- Provide music for dancing.

Developing imagination and imaginative play

A well-designed garden can offer a sense of freedom and privacy for children to play freely and explore their own creativity.

- Use large shrubs or trees to create natural hiding places or dens.
- Alternatively set up a den or 'hidey hole' with a resource box used in conjunction with a high hook on a wall or post.
- A den in a bush will be revisited by children day after day and sometimes they can leave their own play materials there overnight, thus sustaining and extending play.
- Ensure children can access a range of natural materials such as seed heads, conkers, fir cones, etc., which can be used in imaginative play.
- Provide a gravel bed or rockery planted with tough plants or conifers. Small world play becomes more exciting. A large gravel bed can be used with drain pipes and planks to extend play with cars and diggers.
- A garden shed or a trellis arbour can be used as a role play area for an outdoor shop, garage, garden centre, café, vet or whatever the children are interested in at the time.

Observation

One of the joys of working outside with young children is that you never know quite what to expect. Rather like the weather, no two days are the same.

Case study

After a rather long, cold and grey winter we were suddenly experiencing in April clear blue skies and warm sunshine. Daffodils were still in flower, trees in blossom and birds were singing. There was an intensity of light that seemed to bathe everything in clarity and freshness of colour. Even more special was the fact that for once we could appreciate the sounds around us, as all air traffic had been suspended because of a cloud of volcanic ash from Iceland.

I talked about this to a group of children, hoping to draw them into the beauty of the moment.

However, one of the older members of the group said very firmly, 'But I need to get to Canada!' There was only one answer and together we set about building a plane. Children used blocks, logs and some small chairs. The 'pilot' climbed in, but then another child said, 'It's a long way. We need food.' The pilot climbed out again and together the children collected fir cones and leaves using small baskets, which had been provided nearby. The baskets were carefully laid in rows under the chairs. 'We need something to do' said another child and ran off to fetch several books, which he solemnly handed out to the passengers.

I was allowed to board too and we sat one behind the other. The flight lasted for several minutes and during that time each child, including a two-and-a-half-year-old, looked at their book. We duly arrived and after walking round Canada, it was time to come home and again we looked at our books for the duration of the flight.

This observation shows how quickly children's thinking can move and how having appropriate resources available enables so many areas of the curriculum to be explored. In terms of assessment and record keeping, the significant achievement that day was for the youngest child, when he held a book the right way up, turned the pages and concentrated on the content. This child was not able to sit for long in a group at story time, and did not usually access books. He was, however, totally at ease and confident within this group of children as they played outside, enabling him to develop his skills within the context of this role-play situation. It was not something the adult had planned and frequently one looks only in a book corner for chances to assess this area of learning.

Conclusion

Having a garden where children feel confident and at ease will encourage them to develop their own learning scenarios. Adults need to be creative in their thinking not only about the design of the spaces for their children, but also in how they support and develop children's play. They, too, need to become excited and respond to the ever-changing rhythms and patterns of the nursery garden on a daily basis. They will be with the children as they find a frog, watch ice crystals melting or discover the first snowdrop of the year. They will observe children at play and make suggestions or provide resources so that children can develop their thinking and extend their play. There will be planned activities on some days when children and adults work together to sow seeds, plant bulbs or dig up potatoes, but there will be many days when the impact of the garden itself and what it contains will also extend children's learning.

Further reading and useful resources

Bilton H. (2005) *Learning Outdoors*. Abingdon: David Fulton.

DCSF (2008) 'Every Child a Talker: Guidance for Early Language Lead Practitioners' (p. 15). London: The National Strategies. Available online at www.standards.dcsf.gov.uk/nationalstrategies

DCSF (2009) 'Children Thinking Mathematically. PSRN Essential Knowledge for Early Years Practitioners'. London: National Strategies: Available as a download only, online at www.standards.dcsf.gov.uk/nationalstrategies

Conclusion

Through writing this book, I have become even more aware of the importance of 'getting it right' for our youngest children. There are growing concerns that many children are now spending more time in front of a screen rather than using opportunities for exploration, adventure and discovery close at hand in the outdoor environment. We are starting to realize the calming effects of plants and trees as more and more gardens are being built in our hospitals and care homes. It seems that the world of plants offers us a means of escape from the stresses and pressure of everyday adult life. So too for our children. They need to find places to relax, to play and develop their imagination.

There is also increasing evidence of our commitment to world issues of sustainability and conservation. Again, it is the nursery garden that should provide the starting point as children learn to collect rainwater, recycle materials and grow their own food crops. They will develop an awareness of the wildlife and discuss ways of ensuring continuity of species. Many common bird species are declining and by planting hedgerows and food plants, or offering nesting sites and feeders, children become interested and excited about these issues. It is this excitement that will enable them, as adults, to take responsibility for conservation and, in turn, pass their knowledge on to their children.

The nursery garden offers a secure space but it needs to be exciting and challenging. If we can really engage young children in the garden from the beginning, they will develop skills and interests that should sustain them and offer alternative ways to spend their time in later life. There is a wide range of provision for children and some settings are richly endowed with space, and others have no space they can call their own. Hopefully, this book will enable all practitioners to make a critical assessment of what they have and think creatively about what they can achieve.

We need to realize that, as Grace Owen first suggested in 1920 (pp. 144–5):

The consideration of the garden is a matter of supreme importance. It is difficult to overestimate the national importance of a wise provision for the needs of little children.

Bibliography

Bilton, H. (ed.) (2005) *Learning Outdoors*. Abingdon: David Fulton (reprinted 2008).

Clark, A. and Moss, P. (2001) *Listening to Young Children: The Mosaic Approach*. London: National Children's Bureau (reprinted 2005).

Cunningham, S. (2009) *Asian Vegetables: A Guide to Growing Fruit, Vegetables and Spices from the Indian Subcontinent*. Bath: Eco-logic Books.

De Lissa, L. (1939) *Life in the Nursery School*. London: Longmans.

Department for Education, The National Strategies (2008) 'The Early Years Foundation Stage: Setting the Standards for Learning, Development and Care for Children from Birth to Five'. Statutory Framework for the Early Years Foundation Stage (EYFS). Reading: Department for Education and Skills. Ref: 00261-2008PCK-EN. Page 21 in Statutory Framework document.

Department of Education, The National Strategies (2008) 'Every Child a Talker: Guidance for early Language Lead Practitioners'. Ref: 00852008DOM-EN. Pages 15 and 17.

Edwards, C., Gandini, L. and Forman, G. (1998) *The Hundred Languages of Children: The Reggio Emilia Approach Advanced Reflections*. Greenwich: Ablex.

Froebel, F. (1899) *Education by Development*. London: Edward Arnold.

Isaacs, S. (1954) *The Educational Value of the Nursery School*. London: Headley.

Kirby, M. (1989) 'Nature as Refuge in Children's Environments'. *Children's Environments Quarterly*, 6(1): 7–12.

Knight, S. (2009) *Forest Schools and Outdoor Learning in the Early Years*. London: Sage.

Laevers, F., Daems, M., De Bruyckere, G., Declercq, B., Moons, J., Silkens, K., Snoeck, G., Van Kessel, M. (2005) *Well-being and Involvement in Care: A Process Oriented Self-evaluation Instrument for Care Settings*. Leuven University, Belgium: Centre for Experiential Education. Available online at www.kindengezin.be/Images/ZikohandleidingENG_tcm149-50761.pdf

Learning through Landscapes (2008) 'Boys and the Outdoors'. *Playnotes*. For members, available online at www.ltl.org.uk

Louv, R. (2005) *Last Child in the Woods: Saving our Children from Nature Deficit Disorder.* New York: Algonquin Books.

McMillan, M. (1919) *The Nursery School.* London: Dent.

McMillan, M. (*c.*1923) 'What the Open Air Nursery School Is'. *The Labour Party.* London: Transport House.

McMillan, M. (1930) 'The Open Air Nursery School', *New Era*, 11(47): 134–40.

Michie, C. and Bangalor, S. (2010) 'Managing Vitamin D Deficiency in Children', *London Journal of Primary Care*, Aug 10(1): 31–6.

Moore, R. C. (1989) 'Plants as Play Props', *Children's Environments Quarterly*, 6(1): 1–6.

Ouvry, M. (2005) *Exercising Muscles and Minds: Outdoor Play and the Early Years Curriculum.* London: National Children's Bureau.

Ouvry, M. (2009) *Outdoors for Everyone: Enjoying Outdoor Play in the Early Years.* CD-Rom issued by Learning through Landscapes as part of their toolkit 'Outdoors for Everyone'.

Owen, G. (1920) *Nursery School Education.* London: Methuen and Co.

Parry, M. and Archer, H. (1975) *Two to Five, Schools Council Preschool Education Project.* London: McMillan.

Sobel, D. (1990) 'A Place in the World: Adults' Memories of Childhood's Special Places', *Children's Environments Quarterly*, 7(4): 5–12.

Sobel, D. (2002) *Children's Special Places – Exploring the Role of Forts, Dens and Bush Houses in Middle Childhood.* Detroit, MI: Wayne State University.

Tizard, B., Philips, J. and Plewis, I. (1976) 'Play in Preschool Centres –II. Effects on Play of the Child's Social Class and of the Educational Orientation of the Centre', *Journal of Child Psychology and Psychiatry*, 17(4): 265–74.

Tovey, H. (2007) *Playing Outdoors: Spaces and Places, Risk and Challenge.* London: Oxford University Press. This is well worth reading at the beginning of your project as you consider the benefits of outdoor play and what you would like to offer your children.

White, R. (2008) *Benefits for Children of Play in Nature.* Available online at www. whitehutchinson.com/children/articles/benefits.shtml

White, R. and Stoeklin, V. (1998) 'Children's Outdoor Play and Learning Environments: Returning to Nature', *Early Childhood Magazine*, March/ April. Available online at www.whitehutchinson.com/children/articles/ outdoor

www.communityplaythings.org. Download 'I Made a Unicorn'.

www.playengland.org.uk. Download the leaflet 'Managing Risk in Play Provision'.

Index of plants